MW00912543

ACCESS 2.0®
FOR WINDOWS™

Sarah E. Hutchinson
Stacey C. Sawyer
Glen J. Coulthard

THE IRWIN ADVANTAGE SERIES
FOR COMPUTER EDUCATION

◆

IRWIN

BURR RIDGE, ILLINOIS
BOSTON, MASSACHUSETTS
SYDNEY, AUSTRALIA

Printed in the United States of America.

ISBN 0-256-17606-X

Access is a registered trademark of Microsoft Corporation.
Windows graphical environment is a registered trademark of Microsoft Corporation.

3 4 5 6 7 8 9 0 ML 1 0 9 8 7 6 5

Contents

iii

SESSION 2
ACCESS 2.0 FOR WINDOWS: WORKING WITH TABLES   41

SESSION 3
ACCESS 2.0 FOR WINDOWS: RETRIEVING INFORMATION   87

SESSION 4
ACCESS 2.0 FOR WINDOWS: PRESENTING YOUR DATA   123

SESSION 5
ACCESS 2.0 FOR WINDOWS: ADVANCED TOPICS   155

USING THIS GUIDE

This tutorial is one in a series of learning guides that lead you through the most popular microcomputer software programs available. Concepts, skills, and procedures are grouped into session topics and are presented in a logical and structured manner. Commands and procedures are introduced using hands-on examples, and you are encouraged to perform the steps along with the guide. Although you may turn directly to a later session, be aware that some sessions require, or at least assume, that you have completed the previous sessions. For maximum benefit, you should work through the short-answer and hands-on exercises appearing at the end of each session.

The exercises and examples in this guide use several standard conventions to indicate menu instructions, keystroke combinations, and command instructions.

MENU INSTRUCTIONS

When you need to execute a command from a menu, the tutorial's instruction line uses a comma to separate menu options. For example, the command for saving a file is shown as:

CHOOSE: File, Save

This instruction tells you to press the F key to choose the File option and then the S key to choose the Save option. Keys separated by commas are not pressed at the same time.

KEYSTROKES AND KEYSTROKE COMBINATIONS

When you must press two keys together, the tutorial's instruction line shows the keys joined with a plus sign (+). For example, to move the cursor a screen to the right, hold down (Shift) and then press (Tab). The instruction for using this command is shown as:

PRESS: (Shift)+(Tab)

COMMAND INSTRUCTIONS

This guide indicates with a special typeface data that you are required to type in yourself. For example:

TYPE: `George Washington`

When you are required to enter unique information, such as the current date or your name, the instructions appear in italics. The following instruction directs you to type your name in place of the actual words: "your name."

TYPE: *your name*

Instructions that use general directions rather than a specific option or command name appear italicized in the regular typeface.

PRESS: *the cursor-movement keys to highlight the print block*

MICROSOFT ACCESS 2.0 FOR WINDOWS: FUNDAMENTALS

Modern database management systems for microcomputers enable you to store and manage large amounts of data. Whether your computer is used to track inventory products, issue invoices, manage personnel records, or store phone numbers, you will find a computerized database management system a welcome addition to your software library. This session introduces you to the fundamentals of working with Microsoft Access for Windows, a powerful database management application.

PREVIEW

When you have completed this session, you will be able to:

Describe the features of a database management system.
•
Load Windows and start Access for Windows.
•
Open a database and edit a table.
•
Use the UNDO command to reverse editing mistakes.
•
Use the Microsoft Access Help facility.
•
Copy, rename, and delete database objects.
•
Exit Access and Windows.

Why Is This Session Important?
What Is a Microsoft Access Database?
Working with Microsoft Access
       Tables
       Queries
       Forms
       Reports
       Macros
       Modules
The Windows Advantage
Starting Access for Windows
       How the Mouse Is Used in Access
The Guided Tour
       Application Window
       Database Window
       Menu Bar
       Tool Bar
       Status Bar
       Dialog Box
Opening a Database
       Using Datasheet View
The UNDO Command
Selecting Table Data and Editing
       When Does Access Save Your
          Changes?
       Deleting an Existing Record
Getting Help
Managing Database Objects
Closing a Database Window
Exiting Access
Summary
       Command Summary
Key Terms
Exercises
       Short Answer
       Hands-On

WHY IS THIS SESSION IMPORTANT?

This guide leads you step-by-step through using Microsoft Access for Windows, a very powerful relational database management package. Aside from using Access to store and manage large amounts of information, you can query the database for specific information, and create custom forms, labels, reports, and independent applications. By the completion of this guide, you will have the fundamental skills for working with Access.

In Session 1, you learn how to load Microsoft Access, navigate around the database window, view and edit a database, and access the Help facility. After creating a database in Session 2, you add records to a table, view the table, and then modify the table structure. Session 3 introduces querying the database for specific data and linking databases. Session 4 provides lessons for presenting information using custom reports and mailing labels. Session 5 discusses some advanced topics including graphics, file management, and programming.

In order to run Microsoft Access for Windows, your computer system must have the following:
- 80386 (or higher) microprocessor (a minimum speed of 20 megahertz is recommended)
- 19 megabytes free on the hard disk for a typical installation
- At least 6 megabytes of random access memory (RAM); 8 megabytes is recommended
- EGA or VGA display (VGA or higher is recommended)
- A mouse

In the next few sections, before loading Access, we will familiarize you with fundamental database concepts and terminology.

Before proceeding, make sure the following are true:

1. You have access to Microsoft Access 2.0 for Windows.
2. Your Advantage Diskette is inserted into either drive A: or drive B:. You will save your work onto the diskette and open files that have been created for you. (*Note*: The Advantage Diskette can be duplicated by copying all the files from your instructor's Master Advantage Diskette.)

WHAT IS A MICROSOFT ACCESS DATABASE?

Picture an office with a row of file cabinets that extends as far as you can see—and you're responsible for them! Each filing cabinet has multiple folders containing customer-related information, organized in alphabetical order by surname. Everything is perfectly organized and you know exactly where to look to find information on each customer. Great. But what if you need to pull out all folders that contain information on customers who live in Boston? Or produce a list of all customers who haven't purchased anything in the past six months? Your alphabetical organization scheme is no longer useful. Your manual filing system has many limitations of which you are becoming quite aware. You need a microcomputer database management system! A **database management system (DBMS)** is a software tool that facilitates creating and maintaining an information database and producing reports from it. The term **database** describes a collection of data stored for a variety of business purposes.

As with any software package, you must be familiar with the concepts and features of a DBMS before you can use it productively. In defining these concepts, we will use the analogy of a phone book. Make sure that you are comfortable with the following terms:

- *Database*: A collection of related information. For example, a phone book is a database of names, addresses, and phone numbers. Although the term database is often used to refer to a data file, in Microsoft Access a database includes a collection of *objects*—data tables (described shortly), queries, reports, forms, and other objects. In Access, an **object** is something that you can select and manipulate as a unit.

  In Access, all the tables in a database, as well as its associated objects, are stored in a single file that has the extension of MDB. When you open a Microsoft Access database, you're not only opening the data table, you're also making available all the tools (objects) that will help you to use the information stored in the data table. We describe Access objects in more detail shortly. (*Note*: When you create a database, Access also creates an LDB file with the same filename; in multiuse environments, this file contains locking information. You don't need to worry about backing this file up when you copy the database.)

- *Table*: A Microsoft Access object that is used to collect data relating to a particular subject. In Access, tables are organized into columns and rows. A table is analogous to a data file. For example, phone book data would be stored in a table. We describe tables in more detail shortly.

- *Record*: An individual entry in a table. For example, each person's name, address, and phone number are a single record in a phone book. A record of data represents a row in a table.

- *Field*: A piece of information in a record. For example, you can divide a person's record in the phone book into fields for last name, first name, address, city, and phone number. A record is composed of fields. A field is a column in a table.

A database application is any task that would be handled manually using a filing cabinet. A computerized DBMS is preferable to a manual filing system when there are many records to store, update, or summarize, and there are many details or fields for each record. The primary purpose of a DBMS is to translate large amounts of raw data into accurate, relevant, and well-organized information.

There are two distinct types of DBMS software available: relational and flat-file. A **relational database program** allows you to work with several database files at the same time and share information. To implement an accounting database system, for example, you require relational capabilities to link together information in the various ledger files. A **flat-file database program**, on the other hand, allows you to create many databases but only work with one file at a time. Using a flat-file database program, you can create simple applications such as a mailing list database or a personnel file. Microsoft Access is a relational database package.

WORKING WITH MICROSOFT ACCESS

A Microsoft Access database employs tables as the primary element for storing and manipulating information. Each table has an associated family of objects, including queries, forms, reports, macros, and modules. Each of these objects, including tables, is described in more detail below. An Access database can be up to 1 gigabyte (billion bytes) in size.

TABLES

A table is used to collect data on a particular subject. You can use many tables in a database, each used to store data on a different subject. If you create a database that contains many tables, you should plan the database design carefully. We discuss database design considerations in Session 2.

As we described earlier, a table is organized into rows and columns, similarly to a spreadsheet. Each row in a table represents an individual record, while each column represents a field or category of information. The following is an example of a very small table that stores phone information:

Firstname	Middle Initial	Lastname	Address	Phone
Rod	J.	Bannister	7279 Ridge Drive	221-2441
Evelyn	P.	Chabot	2613 Henderson Hiway	221-5000
Michael	W.	Antonucci	4901 101st Place SW	222-1000
Karen		Shepherd	3107 Peachtree Drive	205-2111
Arthur	K.	Sotak	1217 Carlisle Road	221-8888

In Session 2 you learn how to create the structure for a table and add data to it.

QUERIES

A **query** is a question you ask of your database and the result of a query is a **dynaset**. For example, when using a database that stores customer data, you might query the database for a list of those individuals who live in Chicago. The resulting list of records (representing those individuals who live in Chicago) is the dynaset. The data that answers the query, or question, can be from more than one table.

The main difference between a table and a query or dynaset is that data is actually stored (on a disk) in tables, but isn't in queries or dynasets. You learn how to create queries in Session 3.

FORMS

When you view the records in a database, Access displays many records on the screen at once in a table layout. This mode is fine if you want to view many records at once. Forms and reports enable you to customize the way the data stored in tables is displayed. (*Note*: Reports are described in the next section.)

A **form** enables you to view one record on the screen at once and to customize the display of that record. For example, you can include a list of values to choose from, use colors to emphasize important data, and display error messages when incorrect data is entered. Figure 1.1 provides an example of a form that you might use with a phone database.

Figure 1.1

A sample form

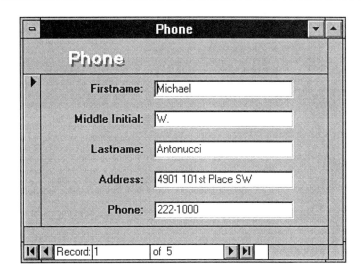

The different elements on a form are called **controls**. Using a control you can display data from a field, the result of a calculation, text for a title or message, a graph, or other object. Controls are also used in reports. You learn how to create forms in Session 2.

REPORTS

Reports are used to present table data in a polished format on the printed page. With a report you can include totals, subtotals, and grand totals across a set of records and tables. Like forms, controls are used to represent the different elements in a report. Figure 1.2 shows a report that is sorted into order by the Lastname field and excludes the Middle Initial and Address fields.

Figure 1.2

A sample report

Phone Numbers

24-May-94

Firstname	Lastname	Phone
Michael	Antonucci	222-1000
Rod	Bannister	221-2441
Evelyn	Chabot	221-5000
Karen	Shepherd	205-2111
Arthur	Sotak	221-8888

You learn how to create reports in Session 4.

MACROS

Using a **macro**, you can automate frequently-performed procedures. For example, when you open a database, you might also want Access to open a form. Or you may want to include a command button on a form that performs a particular function, such as printing a dynaset. We lead you through creating command buttons in Session 5.

MODULES

Macros and other objects provide you with a lot of control over your interaction with a database. For even more control, use **Access Basic**, the programming tool that is included in the Access package. A **module** is an object that contains Access Basic programming instructions, or procedures. You can create a module that will, for example, print a dynaset over and over until a condition you set is true. In this learning guide, we don't lead you through creating modules, but it is important that you know this powerful capability exists.

THE WINDOWS ADVANTAGE

With over 10 million copies sold in the last few years, Windows is fast becoming the environment of choice for many personal computer users. This section explains some of the benefits and shortcomings of working in the Windows environment.

Microsoft Windows is a software package that works with DOS to provide a **graphical user interface (GUI)** for programs. This GUI interface is designed to make using computers easier and more intuitive. With Windows, you use a pointing device called a **mouse** to select from **icons** (pictures that represent programs or functions) rather than typing lengthy commands. However, Windows is not simply another shell to hide you from the unforgiving world of **DOS**. The Microsoft mandate for Windows is to provide a standardized interface for all programs, whether they are word processing, spreadsheet, or database applications. In other words, once you have learned one Windows product, you can use that knowledge in working with other Windows products.

Some other advantages of working in the Windows environment are these:

1. *The ability to run more than one application at a time.*
   Windows is a **multitasking** environment whereby more than one application or program may be run at the same time. This feature is especially important for electronic mail, modem, or fax programs that must be loaded in the computer's memory to inform you of incoming transactions while you are working on something else—adding data to a database, for example. Multitasking allows you to simultaneously look at a database or spreadsheet in one application while working in another.

2. *The ability to exchange information among applications.*
   Windows provides a program called the **Clipboard** to copy and move information within an application or among applications. Because more than one application can be running at the same time, you can, for instance, copy data from an Excel spreadsheet to the ClipBoard and then paste that data into an Access database.

3. *The ability to link or embed objects from one application into another.*
   The latest products being released for Microsoft Windows, including Microsoft Access for Windows, have the ability to integrate applications using a feature called **OLE** (pronounced olé) or Object Linking and Embedding. This feature enables you to embed an object

created using one application into another application. An object may be a table or report, for example. The purpose for embedding objects is to share information.

4. *The ability to display on the screen what you will get from the printer.* This feature is called **WYSIWYG** ("What You See Is What You Get") and allows different fonts, borders, and graphics to be displayed on the screen at all times. Most DOS programs provide a print preview feature but do not display the true WYSIWYG capabilities of Windows programs.

The primary disadvantage of working in the Windows environment is that the program requires a powerful computer to maintain a reasonable processing speed.

STARTING ACCESS FOR WINDOWS

Because Microsoft Windows requires a hard disk, this session assumes that you are working on a computer with DOS, Windows, and Microsoft Access for Windows loaded on the hard disk drive. In most cases, the hard disk of a personal computer is drive C:. The Windows program is stored in a directory on the hard disk called \WINDOWS, much like a reserved drawer in a filing cabinet.

Before using Access, you must turn on the computer and load Microsoft Windows. Perform the following steps on your computer to begin working with Access for Windows:

1. Turn on the power switches to the computer and monitor. The C:\> prompt or a menu appears announcing that your computer has successfully loaded the Disk Operating System (DOS). (*Note*: If your computer automatically loads Microsoft Windows when it is started, you can move on to step 3.)

2. To start Microsoft Windows from the C:\> prompt:
    TYPE: WIN
    PRESS: Enter
    After a few seconds, the Windows logo appears on the screen followed by the Program Manager window (Figure 1.3). (*Note*: The icons in your Program Manager window may not be exactly the same as in Figure 1.3; the icons represent the programs stored on your hard disk.)

3. To start Access for Windows from the Program Manager, first open the Microsoft Access group in the **Program Manager** window:
    DOUBLE-CLICK: *Microsoft Access group icon*

4. Load Access from the Microsoft Access group window (Figure 1.4):
    DOUBLE-CLICK: *Microsoft Access program icon*

Figure 1.3

The Microsoft
Windows Program
Manager

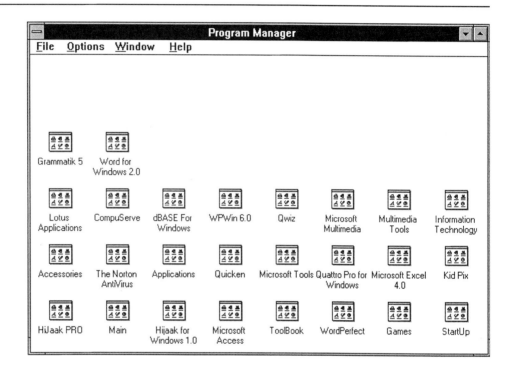

Figure 1.4

The Microsoft
Access group
window

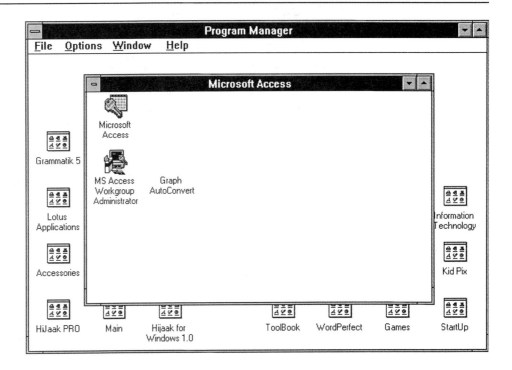

1. To start Windows from the C:\> prompt:
2. TYPE: WIN and then press **Enter**.
3. To start Microsoft Access for Windows from the Program Manager:
   Double-click on the Microsoft Access group icon and then double-click on the Microsoft Access program icon.

HOW THE MOUSE IS USED IN ACCESS

The mouse is an essential tool for working with Microsoft Access for Windows. The mouse actions used in Access are click, double-click, and drag:

- Click   Press down and release the left mouse button quickly. Clicking is used to position the cursor and to choose options from a dialog box.

- Double-Click   Press down and release the left mouse button twice in rapid succession. Double-clicking is often used to select and execute an action.

- Drag   Press down and hold the left mouse button as you move the mouse pointer across the screen. When the mouse pointer reaches the desired location, release the mouse button. Dragging is used to select a block of text or to move items or windows.

You may notice that the mouse pointer changes shape as you move the mouse over different parts of the screen. Each mouse pointer shape has its own purpose and may provide you with important information. There are three primary mouse pointer shapes:

↖	Left arrow	Used to choose menu items or make selections from the Menu bar, Tool bar, and dialog boxes.
⧗	Hourglass	Used to inform you that Access is occupied with another task and to request that you wait.
I	I-beam	Used to modify and edit text, and to position the cursor.

As you proceed through this guide, other mouse shapes will be explained as they appear.

THE GUIDED TOUR

Software programs designed for Microsoft Windows, such as WordPerfect for Windows, Excel, and PageMaker, have many similarities in screen design and layout. Each program operates in its own **Application window** when running under Windows. Within an application, each letter, spreadsheet, or brochure that you create appears in its own **Document window**. Access refers to the Document window as the Database window. This section explores the various parts of Microsoft Access for Windows including the tools for manipulating Application and Database windows.

APPLICATION WINDOW

When you first load Microsoft Access, you are viewing the Application window (Figure 1.5). The Application window consists of the Application Control menu, Minimize and Maximize icons, Title bar, Menu bar, and Status bar.

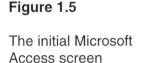

Figure 1.5

The initial Microsoft
Access screen

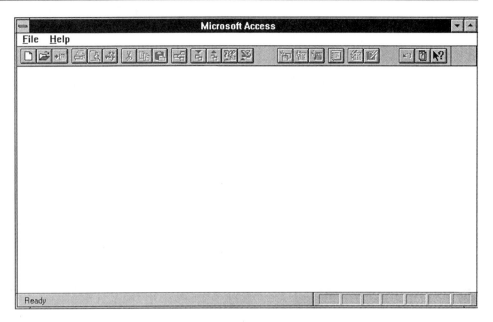

The Application Control menu (═) appears as a small horizontal bar in
the top left-hand corner of the Application window. Accessed by pointing
to it and clicking once (or by holding down **Alt** and pressing the Space
Bar), the Application Control menu is used to size and position the
Application window. To quit Microsoft Access, double-click on the
Application Control menu.

The Minimize (▼) and Maximize (▲) icons are located in the top right-
hand corner of the Application window. These triangular-shaped icons are
used to control the size of the Application window using the mouse.
Applications are often minimized from view when they are not currently
needed but must remain running.

The Title bar, located at the top of the Application window, contains the
name *Microsoft Access*. The Title bar is used to differentiate the active or
current Application window, which has a solid Title bar, from a nonactive
Application window. Using a mouse, you can move the Application
window (when it is not maximized) by dragging its Title bar.

The Menu bar appears on the second line from the top and contains the
names of the different categories of Access commands. When a command
is chosen, a pull-down menu of additional commands becomes available,
such as commands for opening and closing documents, copying and
moving information, and printing. The Menu bar is accessed by clicking
on the command using the mouse. When you first load Microsoft Access,

the Menu bar contains two options: File and Help. We describe the Menu bar in more detail shortly.

The Status bar is located in the bottom row of the Application window and provides information about current activities. The Status bar is described in more detail shortly.

DATABASE WINDOW

When you open a database, Microsoft Access displays a Database window. (*Note*: You learn how to open a database later in this session.) The Database window is your command center; it provides the means to create, view, and edit database objects. When Access is first loaded, no Database window is displaying. When you open a database, it opens into a Database window. Figure 1.6 shows the screen after the TRAINING database was opened.

Figure 1.6

The Database window for the TRAINING database has been opened.

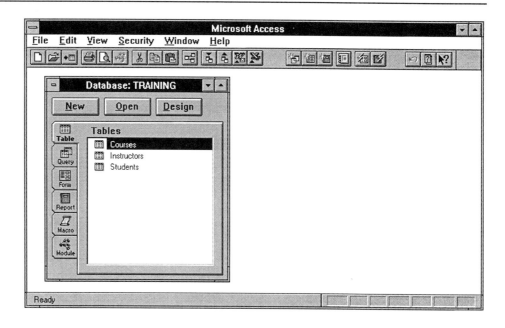

The Database window contains the Database Control menu (▬), which appears as a small horizontal bar in the upper-left corner of the Database window. Accessed by pointing to it and clicking once, the Control menu is used to size and position the Database window. Like in the Application window, the Minimize (▾) and Maximize (▴) icons are located in the top right-hand corner of the Database window.

Object buttons are listed on the left side of the Database window. You use these buttons to tell Access what type of object you want to create or work with. The current assumption is that you want to work with a Table; three table names (Courses, Instructors, Students) are listing to the right. (*Note*: Most databases contain more than one data table.) If you select the Query object button, a list of query objects will list to the right, and so on. We lead you through using the Database window shortly.

The Database window also provides you with three processing buttons. The New button is used when you want to create a new database object. Use the Open button to call up the specifications for an already-created database object, or double-click the database object you want to work with. Use the Design button to change the specifications for a particular object. You will use these buttons in Session 2.

To close a database, choose Close from the File menu or simply double-click the Control menu (in the Database window) using a mouse.

MENU BAR

As described earlier, commands are grouped together on the Menu bar, located at the top of the Application window. The Menu bar changes to display commands and options that are relevant to the current database window. For example, when you first loaded Access, only two options were available on the Menu bar. After you open a database, additional options become available in the Menu bar (see Figure 1.6). To execute a command, first select an option from the Menu bar and then choose a command from the pull-down menu.

The commands on the pull-down menu that are not available for selection appear dimmed. Commands that require further information before execution are followed by an ellipsis (...). This additional information is usually collected in a **dialog box**, which is used to display messages or ask you to confirm commands. (Dialog boxes are described in more detail shortly.)

To access the menu and execute a command using a mouse, click once on the Menu bar option to display the pull-down menu. From the pull-down menu, click once on the command you want to execute. Another way to select a command is to click on the menu option and then drag the mouse pointer down the pull-down menu to the desired command. When the command is highlighted, release the mouse button to execute it.

To execute a command using the keyboard, press and hold down (Alt) and then tap the underlined letter of the desired option on the Menu bar. When the pull-down menu is displayed, press the underlined letter of the command you want to execute. Commands appear in this guide in the following form: Edit, Copy, where Edit is the Menu bar option and Copy is the command to be selected from the pull-down menu. (*Note*: In this guide we assume that your computer is connected to a mouse.)

You can cancel a selection once you are in the Menu bar by pressing (Esc) or by moving the mouse pointer off the menu item and then releasing the mouse button. If you have already executed a command that displays a dialog box, select the Cancel button to abort the procedure.

TOOL BAR

The **Tool bar** provides quick and easy access to the more popular features of Access and displays Help information relating to the current task. Accessible using a mouse, the buttons on the Tool bar provide you with single-step functionality. Like the Menu bar, the Tool bar changes to display different buttons that can be used in the current window. We describe the buttons on the Tool bar as they become relevant.

STATUS BAR

When Access is ready for you to perform an action, the Status bar displays the text "Ready." In general, the **Status bar** displays messages depending on what you are doing in Access. If Access doesn't do what you expect, check the Status bar for messages relating to the current processing task. Also, the Status bar informs you of the status of the CAPS LOCK key (whether it has been pressed or not), NUM LOCK key, and other keyboard keys.

DIALOG BOX

Microsoft Access uses dialog boxes (Figure 1.7) to collect information necessary to execute a command. When a command is followed by an ellipsis (...) on a pull-down menu, Access presents a dialog box upon selection of that command. When a command is followed by a sideways triangle, Access presents another pull-down menu upon selection of the command. As mentioned earlier, dialog boxes are also used to display messages or ask for confirmation of commands.

Figure 1.7

A dialog box

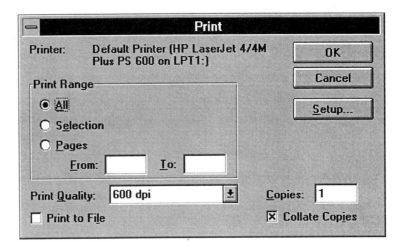

A dialog box uses several methods for collecting information including list boxes, text boxes, drop-down lists, check boxes, option buttons, and command buttons. You activate an item in the dialog box using a mouse, or by pressing Tab to move clockwise and Shift+Tab to move counter-clockwise around the dialog box.

Table 1.1 describes the various methods used for collecting information in dialog boxes.

Table 1.1 Parts of a dialog box	List Box	A scrollable list of choices. Use the scroll bars or cursor keys to browse the list.
	Text Box	A box for collecting typed information. (*Note*: A text box that appears with an arrow to its right can also be used as a drop-down list box.)
	Drop-Down List	A list of available choices in which only one item is displayed at a time. Using a mouse, click on the adjacent arrow to display the full list. Using the keyboard, press Alt+↓ arrow when the box is active (highlighted in reverse video).
	Check Box	An option that can be toggled (switched) on or off. Select the box and press the Space Bar to toggle the "X" mark on and off, or click on the box using a mouse.

Option Button   One option that can be selected from a group of related options.

Command Button   A button that executes an action when selected.

OPENING A DATABASE

To view information in a database you must open it by choosing File, Open or by clicking the Open Database button ([image icon]) on the Tool bar. In this section, we lead you through opening a database file named TRAINING, which is stored on the Advantage Diskette. You will edit a database table, use the UNDO command, display Help information, and close the database. In Session 2 we lead you through creating a database.

Perform the following steps to open the TRAINING database that is stored on the Advantage Diskette:

1. CHOOSE: File, Open Database *from the menu*
   (*Note*: Remember that you can choose options by pointing to them and clicking with the mouse, or by pressing **Alt** and then typing the underlined character of the desired option. Also, some Access procedures can only be performed using a mouse.) The dialog box in Figure 1.8 should be displaying (different files might be listing).

Figure 1.8

The Open Database dialog box

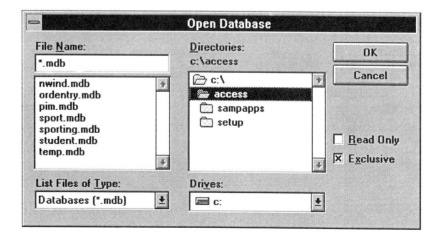

2. Access is currently listing files stored on drive C:. To list the files on the Advantage Diskette that is located in either drive A: or drive B:
    CLICK: in the Drives list box
    CLICK: a: or b: *depending on what drive the Advantage Diskette is in*

3. A list of files stored on the Advantage Diskette should be displaying in the File Name list box.
    SELECT: training.mdb
    PRESS: [Enter] or CLICK: OK
    The TRAINING database has been opened into a Database window.

4. The Table object is the currently selected object. A list of the tables in the TRAINING database is displaying. To see a list of the forms stored in the TRAINING database:
    CLICK: Form button
    A list of the forms should now be displaying in the Database window.

5. To see a list of the reports stored in the TRAINING database:
    CLICK: Report button
    A list of the reports should now be displaying in the Database window.

6. To display the contents of the Instructors table:
    CLICK: Table button
    SELECT: Instructors
    CHOOSE: Open button
    The TRAINING table is loaded into memory and is displaying in **Datasheet view**. In this view mode, the table data is displayed in rows and columns and is referred to as a **datasheet**. You can see more than one record on the screen at once (Figure 1.9). (*Note*: A different number of records might be displaying on your screen.)

Figure 1.9

The Instructors table is displaying in another window.

	Instructor ID	First Name	Last Name	Address	City	State	Z
	AAAA	Eric	Abrahamson	130 Flay Street, #301	S.F.	CA	94308
	BBBB	Brian	Andrews	132 Blue Street	S.F.	CA	94109
	CCCC	Lawrence	Alexander	198 Broad Street, #100	S.F.	CA	94109
	DDDD	Kirk	Andrews	226 Valley Street	S.F.	CA	94121
	EEEE	Mark	Anderson	1459 River Drive	Houston	TX	77079
	FFFF	Victoria	Bowman	20 Spruce Avenue	San Mateo	CA	94010
	GGGG	Arthur	Mikowski	12 Elm Circle	Sacramento	CA	95825
	HHHH	Ibrahim	Brown	177 Forest Avenue	San Mateo	CA	94010
	IIII	Audrey	Koh	347 Glen	Alta Dena	CA	91001
	JJJJ	James	Barnes	8 Shane Drive	Moraga	CA	94556
	KKKK	Paul	Jemelian	P.O. Box 12	Burlingame	CA	94010
	LLLL	Bruce	Callander	2 Kron Lane	S.F.	CA	94131
	MMMM	Carl	Costigan	29 Glen Jane	Ventura	CA	93003
	NNNN	Jorges	Forneau	32 Oaks Drive, #115	Thousand Oaks	CA	91361
	OOOO	John	Callus	P.O. Box 312	Walnut Grove	CA	95690
	PPPP	Li-Hwa	Ling	15997 SE 135th	Clackamas	OR	97015
	QQQQ	Carol	Costigan	2440 Scott Street	S.F.	CA	94115
	RRRR	Peter	Victor	98 Hampton Square	S.F.	CA	94121
	SSSS	Theodore	Caulkins	174 Waverly Avenue	S.F.	CA	94109
	TTTT	Dean	Dennis	619 Lorenzo	Santa Monica	CA	90402
	UUUU	Pablo	Mesias	5 Pepper Avenue	Burlingame	CA	94010

Record: 1 of 26

Quick Reference	1. CHOOSE: File, Open *from the Menu bar, or*
Opening a Database	CLICK: 🖼
	2. If necessary, choose Drives and then select the drive where your files are stored.
	3. SELECT: filename.MDB
	PRESS: Enter or CLICK: OK

USING DATASHEET VIEW

In Datasheet view, each row contains an individual record and each column contains field information. To properly manage a database, you must know how to efficiently move the **cursor** to view all parts of a table. Table 1.2 provides a summary of the cursor-movement keys available in Datasheet view.

Table 1.2	⬆	Move up to previous record
Moving the cursor in Datasheet view	⬇	Move down to next record
	⬅, ➡	When editing, move cursor left or right in a field
	Ctrl+⬅	Move left one field
	Ctrl+➡	Move right one field
	PgUp, PgDn	Move up or down one screen, which equals the size of the Database window
	Home	Move to first field in a record
	End	Move to last field in a record
	Ctrl+Home	Move to the top of a database (first record)
	Ctrl+End	Move to the bottom of a database (last record)

Perform the following steps:

1. To move to the last field, one field at a time:
    PRESS: Ctrl+➡ *repeatedly*
    If you're working with a table that is wider than the screen, the screen will automatically scroll horizontally. After the cursor reaches the last field, it will move to the first field of the second row.

2. To move to the first field in a record:
    PRESS: Home

3. To move down a screen:
    PRESS: PgDn

4. To move to the last field in the database table:
    PRESS: Ctrl+End

5. To move to the beginning of the database table:
    PRESS: Ctrl+Home

6. Keep the Instructors table on the screen. You will edit it shortly.

THE UNDO COMMAND

Before learning how to modify table information, you should be familiar with the **UNDO command** for reversing mistakes made during editing. Access provides two UNDO commands. By choosing Edit, Undo Typing, you can undo the most recent change you made to the data. By choosing Edit, Undo Current Field, you can undo all the changes you made to the current field. Even after you save changes or move to another record, you can undo changes to a previous record by choosing Edit, Undo Saved Record. However as soon as you begin editing another record or move to another window, your changes become permanent. You will use the UNDO command in the next section.

Quick Reference	• CHOOSE: Edit, Undo Typing to reverse the most recent change you
UNDO command	made to data
	• CHOOSE: Edit, Undo Current Field to reverse all the changes you
	made to the current field
	• CHOOSE: Edit, Undo Saved Record to reverse any changes you
	made to a previous record

SELECTING TABLE DATA AND EDITING

When you open a table, the first field in the first record of the table is selected (that is, displaying in inverse video). When you're editing a database, keep the following in mind:

- If you start typing while data is selected, what you type will replace the selected data.

- If the cursor is positioned in a field but no data is selected, what you type will be inserted in the field.

- Press (BackSpace) to delete the character to the left of the cursor and press (Delete) to delete the character at the cursor.

Perform the following steps to practice selecting field and record data in the Instructors table (stored in the TRAINING database), and editing:

1. The Instructors table should be displaying on the screen.
    PRESS: `Ctrl`+`Home`
    The cursor is in the first field of the data table and the data in the field
    ("AAAA") is selected.
    PRESS: `Tab` *twice*
    The cursor is in the Last Name field and the field is selected.
    PRESS: `Shift`+`Tab` *once*
    The cursor has moved to the left one field and the field is selected.

2. To practice deleting text and then using the UNDO command:
    PRESS: `Tab` *until the Address field is selected*
    PRESS: `Delete`
    The Address field should now be empty.

Note that a pencil, called the *pencil indicator*, is displaying on the left side
of the record. This displays next to the record you're editing when editing
changes haven't yet been saved. The pencil indicator will disappear when
you move to another record and the changes to the previous record are
automatically saved. We describe the pencil indicator again in the next
section.

3. To bring the data back:
    CHOOSE: Edit, Undo Delete *from the Menu*
    The Address field should now contain the original data.

You can also select a field by pointing to the left side of the field until you
see a right-pointing arrow and then clicking with the mouse.

1. To select Mark Anderson's Address field, point to the left of the field
    so that a right-pointing arrow displays and then click with the mouse.
    The address should be selected.

2. To edit Audrey Koh's last name so that it is "Moh":
    POINT: *to Audrey Koh's Last Name field*
    Notice that when the mouse pointer is directly over the field, an I-beam
    displays. The **I-beam** marks where you can begin editing once you
    click with the mouse.
    POINT: *to the left of the "K" of "Koh," and then*
    CLICK: *with the mouse*
    The cursor (a vertical bar) should be displaying to the left of the "K."

3. If you press ⬅ and ➡, the cursor will move left and right within the field. To practice:
    PRESS: ➡ *twice*
    PRESS: ⬅ *until the cursor is to the left of "K"*

4. To delete the "K":
    PRESS: [Delete]
    TYPE: M
    "Moh" should now be displaying.

5. POINT: *to a field in another record and then click with the mouse*
    By moving the cursor to another record, the changes you made to the previous record were saved onto the disk.

6. If you decide right now that you shouldn't have changed Audrey Koh's last name:
    CHOOSE: Edit, Undo Saved Record
    "Koh" should now be displaying in the Last Name field.

7. To position the cursor at the top of the table:
    PRESS: [Ctrl]+[Home]

8. Keep the Instructors table on the screen. You will use it in the next few sections.

Quick Reference	To edit the data stored in a field:
Modifying a Table's Field Information	1. Point to the field you want to change (an I-beam should be displaying) and then click with the mouse.
	2. Make your changes. When you click in another record, the changes you made to the previous record are saved.
	To delete the data stored in a field:
	1. POINT: *to the left of the field you want to select until a right-pointing arrow displays and then click with the mouse*
	2. PRESS: [Delete] to delete the selected field
	3. If necessary, choose Edit, Undo to reverse the action.

WHEN DOES ACCESS SAVE YOUR CHANGES?

As you learned in the last section, Access automatically saves your editing changes when you select or click in a different record in the table or close the current window. Therefore, you don't have to use a SAVE command to save table records. When you edit a record, the pointer on the left side of the record changes to a pencil indicator. When you move to another record, the pencil indicator disappears, which means that your changes are saved.

To save the changes you make to a record without moving to a different record, choose File, Save Record.

DELETING AN EXISTING RECORD

While displaying a table in the Datasheet view, delete a record by selecting the record and then pressing (Delete). Access deletes the record but displays a dialog box that lets you reconsider. Choose OK to delete the record or Cancel to restore the record to the database. You can delete a group of records by dragging the mouse in the **record selection area**, which is to the left of the first column in the datasheet.

To select a record, point to the left side of the entire record until the mouse pointer looks like a right-pointing arrow. Click the mouse to select the record. (*Note*: Using the Menu bar, first position the cursor in any field in the record you want to select and then choose Edit, Select Record.)

Perform the following steps:

1. To select the entire second record (describing Brian Andrews), use the mouse to point to the area to the left of the first column (opposite the second record) until a right arrow displays. Then click with the mouse. The entire record should be selected.

2. To delete the selected record:
   PRESS: (Delete)
   The following dialog box should be displaying:

As a word of warning, Access always displays this dialog box when you try to delete a record. If you click OK at this point, the record will be permanently deleted from the database. If you click Cancel, the record will remain in the data table.

3. To keep the selected record in the database:
    CLICK: Cancel button

4. To close the datasheet:
    CHOOSE: File, Close
    The Database window should be displaying.

Quick Reference	1. Select the record you want to delete.
Deleting a Record	2. PRESS: [Delete]
	3. CLICK: OK button *to permanently delete the record, or*
	CLICK: Cancel button *to undelete the record*

GETTING HELP

Access provides reference and "how to" Help information for every Microsoft Access task you can perform. In addition, it includes an alphabetical listing of Access objects, properties, actions, functions, statements, and methods. You can access the Help facility through the Menu bar by choosing Help, or display context-sensitive Help when you press [F1] or click the Help button ([?]) on the Tool bar. *Context-sensitive* refers to Access's ability to retrieve Help information reflecting your current position in the program and your current needs. For other Help, you can use the Help option on the Menu bar; its commands are listed in Table 1.3.

A useful feature of the Microsoft Access Help system is that you can print the Help information you display on the screen by choosing File, Print Topic from the Help window.

Table 1.3	Contents	A list of all the Help sections.
The Help menu	Search	Search for specific topics by typing in keywords. Topics are organized alphabetically.
	Cue Cards	Display an online coach to help you perform database tasks.
	About Microsoft Access	Display version number and system information.

Perform the following steps to access the Help facility through the Menu bar:

1. Choose the Help, Contents command from the menu:
   CHOOSE: Help, Contents
   The Help window should look similar to Figure 1.10. (*Note*: The Help window on your screen may be a different size.)

Figure 1.10

The Help facility. This window was displayed after choosing Help, Contents.

2. To move through the subject areas:
   PRESS: [Tab] *and* [Shift]+[Tab]

3. Position the mouse pointer over the subject areas but do not click the mouse button. Notice that the mouse pointer becomes a hand when moving over the topic areas.

4. To view Help information about Using Microsoft Access (the first option listed vertically on the screen), move the mouse pointer over the topic and click the left mouse button:
   CLICK: Using Microsoft Access

5. As you continue to choose options, additional options become available. To close the window:
CHOOSE: File, Exit, *or*
DOUBLE-CLICK: the Help control menu (➖), located in upper-left corner of the Help screen

Perform the following steps to access context-sensitive help.

1. To access Help from anywhere in the program:
CLICK: ▓

2. Access is waiting for you to point to an object that you want to learn more about.
POINT: at the Database window
CLICK: the left mouse button
Help information relating to the Database window should be displaying.

3. After reading the Help information, close the window:
CHOOSE: File, Exit

To search for information:

1. Let's say you are interested in finding out more about Microsoft Access objects:
CHOOSE: Help, Search
The Search dialog box is displaying.

2. Access is waiting for you to type in a description of what you want to know more about.
TYPE: cue cards
(*Note*: You can type in either upper- or lowercase letters.) The Search dialog box should be displaying a list of topics:

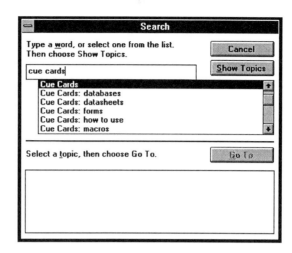

3. To find out more about using Cue Cards:
    SELECT: Cue Cards: how to use
    PRESS: <u>S</u>how Topics
    A list of related topics (in this case, only one topic is displaying) should be displaying on the bottom half of the Search window.
    SELECT: About Cue Cards *on the bottom of the Search window*
    PRESS: <u>G</u>o To
    Information about Microsoft Access Cue Cards is displaying in the Help window.

Remember, you can print the topic information that is displaying in the current window, by choosing <u>F</u>ile, <u>P</u>rint Topic.

4. To close the window:
    CHOOSE: <u>F</u>ile, E<u>x</u>it, *or*
    DOUBLE-CLICK: the Help control menu (▬), located in the upper-left corner of the Help screen.

Quick Reference *Using Help*	• Press F1 or click 🅚? to display context-sensitive Help. • Display the Help menu by choosing Help and then one of the available Help options. • To exit the Help facility, choose <u>F</u>ile, E<u>x</u>it, or double-click the Help control menu (▬) in the upper-left corner of the Help screen.

MANAGING DATABASE OBJECTS

As you proceed with this learning guide, you will create many different database objects, including table, query, form, and report objects, and it is important for you to know how to manage them. In this section, you learn how to copy, rename, and delete database objects; you will find these procedures useful as you proceed with this learning guide.

The TRAINING Database window should be displaying on the screen.

1. To display a list of the reports that are stored in the TRAINING database:
   CLICK: Report button

2. Suppose you want to make a copy of the Instructor Listing report so that you can later edit it to include fewer columns. To copy the report:
   CLICK: Instructor Listing report
   CHOOSE: Edit, Copy
   The report has been copied to the Clipboard.
   CHOOSE: Edit, Paste

3. Access is now waiting for you to type a name for the copied report.
   TYPE: Modified Instructor Listing
   PRESS: (Enter) or CLICK: OK
   The TRAINING Database window should still be displaying on the screen. Notice that the copied report appears in the list of reports.

Quick Reference	1.	Select the object you want to copy.
Copying an Object	2.	CHOOSE: Edit, Copy
	3.	CHOOSE: Edit, Paste
	4.	TYPE: *a name for the copy*
		PRESS: (Enter) or CLICK: OK

To rename an object, select the object and then choose File, Rename from the Menu bar. To illustrate:

1. CLICK: Report button
   SELECT: Modified Instructor Listing object

2. CHOOSE: File, Rename
   TYPE: New Instructor Listing
   PRESS: (Enter) or CLICK: OK
   The object has been renamed.

Quick Reference *Renaming an Object*	1. Select the object you want to rename. 2. CHOOSE: File, Rename 3. TYPE: *a new name* PRESS: [Enter] or CLICK: OK

To delete an object, select the object and then choose Edit, Delete from the Menu bar. To illustrate:

1. CLICK: Report button
    SELECT: New Instructor Listing object

2. CHOOSE: Edit, Delete
    PRESS: [Enter] or CLICK: OK
    The object has been deleted.

Quick Reference *Deleting an Object*	1. Select the object you want to delete. 2. CHOOSE: Edit, Delete PRESS: [Enter] or CLICK: OK

CLOSING A DATABASE WINDOW

When working with Access you will often work with more than one Database window at a time. Often, you will want to close a window because you are no longer using its contents or because you want to clean up the Microsoft Access desktop. To close the current window, choose File, Close or double-click the Database Control menu (▰) in the upper-left corner of the window.

Do the following:

The TRAINING Database window is now displaying. To close this window using the Database Control menu:

DOUBLE-CLICK: ▰ *in the upper-left corner of the window*

The Microsoft Access workspace looks as it did when you first loaded the program. (*Note*: You could have chosen File, Close from the Menu bar.)

Quick Reference Closing a Window	CHOOSE: File, Close, or DOUBLE-CLICK: the Control menu (■)

It is a good idea to close all windows before exiting Microsoft Access, which is described in the next section.

EXITING ACCESS

The procedure required to exit Microsoft Access is identical to that of exiting a window. It is a good idea to exit Microsoft Access at the end of each working session.

Perform the following steps:

1. To exit Microsoft Access for Windows:
    CHOOSE: File, Exit
    The application is closed and you are returned to the Program Manager.

2. To exit Windows:
    CHOOSE: File, Exit
    Note: Rather than using the menu commands, you can double-click the Application Control menu (■) in the upper-left corner to close an application.
    Windows now asks if you really want to exit.
    CLICK: OK

Quick Reference Exiting Access and Windows	1. CHOOSE: File, Exit or double-click Access's Application Control menu (■)
	2. CHOOSE: File, Exit or double-click the Program Manager's Application Control menu (■)

SUMMARY

Microsoft Access is a relational database management system for microcomputers. A database management system enables you to store and manipulate large amounts of data. You create a database application in Access using various types of objects. Information is gathered, stored, and manipulated in tables, the primary element of an Access database.

In this first session, you learned how to open a data table into a window and view information using the Datasheet view. After practicing the cursor-movement keys for traversing a table, you modified field information. You learned that once you begin work on a different record, any changes you made to the previous record are saved. You also learned how to display Help information on the screen.

In the next session you learn how to design a database table and then add data to it.

COMMAND SUMMARY

Many of the commands and procedures appearing in this session are provided in the command summary in Table 1.4.

Table 1.4 Command Summary	*COMMAND*	*TASK*
	File, Open	Open a database.
	Edit, Undo	Reverse your most recent changes.
	Select a record in the datasheet, [Delete]	Delete a record from a datasheet.
	[F1] or [?]	Display context-sensitive Help information on the screen.
	Help	Use the Menu bar to access Help information
	Edit, Copy Edit, Paste	Copy a database object.
	File, Rename	Rename a database object.
	Edit, Delete	Delete a database object.
	File, Close	Close a window.

KEY TERMS

Access Basic   The programming tool that is included in the Microsoft Access package.

Application window   In Microsoft Windows, each running application program appears in its own Application window.

Clipboard   Windows provides a program called the Clipboard to copy and move information within an application or among applications.

controls   The different elements on a form or report.

cursor   The vertical flashing bar that indicates your current position on the screen. The cursor shows where the next typed characters or spaces will appear.

database   A collection of data stored for a variety of business purposes. In Microsoft Access a database includes a collection of *objects*—data tables, queries, reports, forms, and other objects.

database management system (DBMS)   A software tool that facilitates creating and maintaining an information database and producing reports from it.

datasheet   When table data is displayed in rows and columns, it is called a datasheet.

Datasheet view   In this view mode, the table data is displayed in rows and columns and is referred to as a datasheet.

dialog box   A box that displays messages or asks for confirmation of commands.

Document window   In Microsoft Windows, each open document appears in its own Document window. These windows can be sized and moved anywhere within the document area. (A Document window represents your workspace.)

DOS   Acronym for Disk Operating System. Internal command instructions for certain microcomputers.

dynaset   The result of a query.

field   A piece of information in a record.

flat-file database program   A database program that allows you to create many databases but only work with one file at a time.

form   A form enables you to view one record on the screen at once and to customize the display of that record.

graphical user interface   Software feature that allows the user to select menu options and icons instead of remembering complicated command language; makes software easier to use and typically employs a mouse.

I-beam   Marks where you can begin editing once you click with the mouse.

icon   A picture or screen that represents a program or a software function.

macro   Using a macro, you can automate frequently performed procedures.

Microsoft Windows   Graphical user interface software that works with DOS to make it easier for users to run programs.

module   An object that contains Access Basic programming instructions, or procedures.

mouse   Handheld input device connected to a microcomputer by a cable; when the mouse is rolled across the desktop, the cursor moves on the screen. A button on the mouse allows users to make menu selections and to issue commands.

multitasking   Activity in which more than one task or program is executed at one time.

object   Something that you can select and manipulate as a unit.

object buttons   Buttons that appear on the left side of the database window. Use them to select the type of object to work with: table, form, query, report, macro, or module.

OLE   Acronym for Microsoft Windows' Object Linking and Embedding technology. This feature of Windows programs facilitates the exchange of data between applications.

Program Manager   The primary window or shell for Microsoft Windows. Applications are organized and launched from the Program Manager window.

query   A question you ask of your database.

record   An individual entry, or row, in a table.

record selection area   An area to the left of the first column in the datasheet.

relational database program   A database program that allows you to work with several database files at the same time and share information.

reports   Used to present table data in a polished format on the printed page.

Status bar   Displays messages depending on what you are doing in Access.

table   A Microsoft Access object that is used to collect data relating to a particular subject.

Tool bar   The Tool bar displays beneath the Menu bar and provides quick and easy access to the more popular features of Access and displays Help information relating to the current task.

UNDO command   In a software application, a command that reverses, or cancels, the last command executed.

WYSIWYG   Acronym for What You See Is What You Get; page description software that allows the user to see the final version of a document on the screen—including the results of formatting—before it is printed out.

EXERCISES

SHORT ANSWER

1. What is a database management system?
2. Define the following terms: *table*, *record*, and *field*.
3. What is the primary element of a Microsoft Access database application?
4. What is an *object* in Microsoft Access?
5. What is the procedure for deleting a record?
6. Using Microsoft Access, how do you display context-sensitive Help information on the screen?
7. What is a Microsoft Access form? Datasheet?
8. How do you close a Microsoft Access window?
9. What is a query? A dynaset?
10. What is a Microsoft Access macro?

HANDS-ON

(*Note*: We assume that you have completed the material presented in this session. Also, the following exercises should be completed in order.)

1. In this exercise, you practice using the Help facility in Microsoft Access.
   a. Load Microsoft Access.
   b. Search for information on "opening databases." Then display Help information on Opening an Existing Database.
   c. Print the Opening an Existing Database topic out on your printer.
   d. Close the Help window.

2. In this exercise, you will open an existing database, practice moving around a table, and then make editing changes.
   a. Open WEDDING.MDB from the Advantage Diskette that is stored in either drive A: or drive B:.
   b. Open the Guest List table. The datasheet should be displaying on the screen.
   c. Maximize the Guest List table by clicking the maximize (▲) button in the upper-right corner of the window. The datasheet should look similar to Figure 1.11. (*Note*: The Guest List table might be a different size on your computer.)
   d. Move to the last record in the table.
   e. Move to the first record in the table.
   f. Move to the second record.
   g. Move to the last field in the second record.
   h. Move to the first field in the second record.
   i. PRESS: [Tab] *until the cursor is highlighting the First Name field for Brian Andrews*
   TYPE: Robert
   "Robert" should have replaced "Brian."
   j. Click with the mouse in another field; you can hear the computer saving the edited record onto the Advantage Diskette.
   k. To close the Guest List window:
   CHOOSE: File, Close

Figure 1.11
The Guest List table
(partial view)

Guest ID	Number in	Title	First Name	Last Name	Address	City	
1	2	Mr. and Mrs.	Eric	Abrahamson	130 Flay Street, #301	S.F.	CA
2	1	Mr.	Brian	Andrews	132 Blue Street	S.F.	CA
3	2	Mr. and Mrs.	Lawrence	Alexander	198 Broad Street, #100	S.F.	CA
4	1	Mr.	Kirk	Andrews	226 Valley Street	S.F.	CA
5	2	Mr. and Mrs.	Mark	Anderson	1459 River Drive	Houston	TX
6	1	Ms.	Victoria	Bowman	20 Spruce Avenue	San Mateo	CA
7	2	Mr. and Mrs.	Arthur	Mikowski	12 Elm Circle	Sacramento	CA
8	2	Mr. and Mrs.	Ibrahim	Brown	177 Forest Avenue	San Mateo	CA
9	1	Ms.	Audrey	Koh	347 Glen	Alta Dena	CA
10	2	Mr. and Mrs.	James	Barnes	8 Shane Drive	Moraga	CA
11	1	Mrs.	Paul	Jemelian	P.O. Box 12	Burlingame	CA
13	2	Mr. and Mrs.	Bruce	Callander	2 Kron Lane	S.F.	CA
14	2	Mr. and Mrs.	Carl	Costigan	29 Glen Jane	Ventura	CA
15	2	Mr. and Mrs.	Jorges	Forneau	32 Oaks Drive, #115	Thousand Oaks	CA
16	2	Mr. and Mrs.	John	Callus	P.O. Box 312	Walnut Grove	CA
17	2	Mr. and Mrs.	Li-Hwa	Ling	15997 SE 135th	Clackamas	OR
18	1	Mrs.	Carol	Costigan	2440 Scott Street	S.F.	CA
19	2	Mr. and Mrs.	Peter	Victor	98 Hampton Square	S.F.	CA
20	1	Mr.	Theodore	Caulkins	174 Waverly Avenue	S.F.	CA
21	2	Mr. and Mrs.	Dean	Dennis	619 Lorenzo	Santa Monica	CA
22	2	Mr. and Mrs.	Pablo	Mesias	5 Pepper Avenue	Burlingame	CA
23	2	Mr. and Mrs.	William	Darsie	P.O. Box 4	Walnut Grove	CA
24	2	Mr. and Mrs.	William	Dagley	53 Oak Avenue	San Rafael	CA

MICROSOFT ACCESS 2.0 FOR WINDOWS: WORKING WITH TABLES

Not too long ago, computerized databases were managed by programmers and were only found in large organizations. With the advent of database management software for microcomputers, even novice computer users can now store and access vast amounts of information. Microsoft Access, for example, allows you to perform complex database procedures using a few simple keystrokes. This session shows you how to create, modify, organize, and customize the tables in an Access database.

PREVIEW

When you have completed this session, you will be able to:

Design and create a data table.

•

Define and remove primary keys and indexes.

•

Add records to a table.

•

Create a form with the AutoForm Wizard.

•

Customize the datasheet view.

•

Modify the table structure.

•

Print a table.

•

Use the Table Wizard.

SESSION OUTLINE

Why Is This Session Important?
Designing a Database
Creating a Database: Sporting, Inc.
      Creating a Table Structure
      Setting a Primary Key
      Defining and Removing Indexes
Adding Records
Creating a Form with the AutoForm Wizard
Customizing the Datasheet View
      Adjusting the Column Widths
      Adjusting Row Heights
      Changing the Displayed Font
      Reordering Fields
      Saving the Datasheet Layout
Modifying the Table Structure
      Inserting and Deleting Fields
      Setting Field Properties
Printing a Table
      Printing the Datasheet
      Printing the Table Definition
Using the Table Wizard
Summary
      Command Summary
Key Terms
Exercises
      Short Answer
      Hands-On

WHY IS THIS SESSION IMPORTANT?

This session builds upon the fundamental skills that you have already learned, such as opening a database, displaying a datasheet, using the UNDO command, editing, deleting one or more records, and closing a database. In the previous session, you worked with a database that was provided to you on the Advantage Diskette. In this session, you learn how to create your own database, which will include a table that you will create. Later in the session, you will modify the structure of the table. Because not all people want data arranged and displayed in the same way, you are also shown how to customize the way a table looks on the screen.

Before proceeding, make sure the following are true:

1. You have loaded Microsoft Access for Windows.
2. Your Advantage Diskette is inserted into drive A: or drive B:. You will save your work onto the diskette and retrieve files that have been created for you. (*Note*: The Advantage Diskette can be duplicated by copying all the files from your instructor's Master Advantage Diskette.)

DESIGNING A DATABASE

Many people who have worked with databases can attest to the "90/10 rule" of database design. It reads something like this: Spend 90% of your time designing a database in order to spend only 10% of your time maintaining it. As you can probably infer from this rule, many problems arising in database management are traceable to faulty structural designs. This section provides tips for designing a database and putting the 90/10 rule to work.

1. *Determine your output requirements.*
    In order to design a database, you must first state your expectations of the database in terms of the queries and reports desired from the system. For example, what type of reports are you expecting to receive? Are the reports produced daily, weekly, monthly, or annually? When you need access to the data, how will you ask for the information from the database? Will you perform queries based on a part number, surname, pet's birth date, or some other information?

2. *Design your database application on paper.*
   Although our technology-driven society strives towards the paperless office, you still need to use paper to plot the course. Being able to transfer your database concept onto paper proves that you understand the problem or opportunity. This step also ensures that you have a working document or guideline for future reference. You should continually modify and update this document as your needs change.

3. *Divide information into separate fields.*
   In this step, you determine the information to include in the database. To allow the most flexibility in manipulating a table, you want to divide information into separate fields. For example, you typically have two fields for a person's name, First Name and Last Name, in order to sort and query the database using the contents of either field.

4. *Divide the information into separate data tables.*
   When designing a database, you attempt to reduce occurrences where the same information is typed into the same fields in different records. For example, an invoice table with fields for the customer's name and address requires that this information be entered for each invoice. The name and address of a customer invoiced once a week will appear in several records in the same table. To avoid this redundancy, you place the customer information in a separate table and give each customer a unique identification code. In the invoice database, you simply enter the customer's code rather than name and address. The invoice and customer tables are then related to each other based on their common field (customer identification code). Related databases can share information for printing reports and performing queries. This process of dividing redundant information into separate databases is called **normalizing a database**.

5. *Identify each record with a unique code.*
   As discussed in the previous step, you need a unique code to identify records when attempting to establish relationships between databases. This code does not have to have a special meaning attached—a numeric field that is automatically incremented works well. This field usually appears at the top of a table structure.

6. *Place the most important fields at the top of the table structure.*
   After performing the first five steps, you create the structure for the database tables. Because of the way that databases are stored in disk files, you place the most important fields at the top of a table structure to improve performance. Important fields are those fields that are used in sorting and querying the table.

7. *Test your database.*

   After creating a table structure, you should test that database before converting or adding information to the table. Add several records to the database tables and then produce a few reports and queries to see whether the information is easily accessible. From these basic operations, you can usually determine what additional fields are necessary and what fields can be removed to save storage space.

CREATING A DATABASE: SPORTING, INC.

In this section you begin creating a database for Sporting, Inc., a hypothetical sporting goods company based in Chicago, which specializes in selling personalized sporting items to companies around the United States and Canada. Sporting, Inc. puts a company's name, logo, or other information on any sporting item of the company's choice. The company then gives the items to its clients, prospective clients, employees, etc. For example, Sporting, Inc. recently delivered 1000 cans of tennis balls to a company in Southern California with the company's logo printed on each ball.

Remember that a database is a collection of tables, queries, forms, reports, macros, and modules. Before you can design any of these objects, you must give a name to the database that contains them. The name you specify must adhere to DOS's filenaming conventions; that is, the name must be between one and eight characters with no spaces.

In this section, you will begin work on a database system named SPORTING that will keep track of customers, sales representatives, invoices, products, and suppliers for Sporting, Inc. Perform the following steps:

1. The initial Access screen should be displaying and all Database windows should be closed.

2. CHOOSE: File, New Database

3. To create a database that will be stored on the Advantage Diskette in drive A: or drive B:
   CLICK: the Dri_ves_ list box
   CLICK: a: or b: *in the Dri_ves_ list box*

4. In this step you will type a filename into the File _N_ame text box. Unless you type a name, your database will be named DB1.MDB.
   SELECT: the text in the File _N_ame text box
   TYPE: sporting
   PRESS: [Enter] or CLICK: OK
   (*Note*: Access automatically supplies the extension of MDB to your database files.)

The Application window should look similar to Figure 2.1.

Figure 2.1

The SPORTING
Database window
doesn't yet contain
any objects.

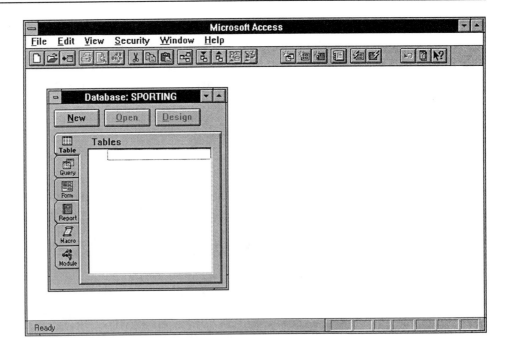

You must create one or more tables before you can create any other database object because tables form the basis of all your queries, forms, and reports. In the next section we lead you through designing the structure for a table that will store information on each of Sporting, Inc.'s customers.

Quick Reference *Creating a New* *Database*	1. CHOOSE: <u>F</u>ile, New <u>D</u>atabase 2. SELECT: a drive *from the Dri<u>v</u>es list box* 3. TYPE: a filename *into the File <u>N</u>ame text box* PRESS: Enter or CLICK: OK 4. From here, you create tables and other database objects (described in later sessions).

CREATING A TABLE STRUCTURE

To create a table in Access, you define a table structure that contains the field names and data types for storing information. You define the new structure by clicking the <u>N</u>ew button in the Database window. The name of the new table is TABLE1 until you save the new table and give it a different name. The new table is saved into the SPORTING.MDB file. When naming the new table, you don't have to adhere to DOS's filenaming conventions because the table isn't stored in a separate file. Specifically, when naming tables and other database objects, you can use up to 64 characters, including spaces.

Perform the following steps to create a table named Customers in the SPORTING file:

1. The SPORTING Database window should be displaying and the Table button is selected (by default).
   CLICK: <u>N</u>ew

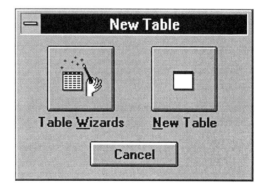

At this point, you have the choice of either creating the table structure from scratch or using a **Table Wizard** to simplify the process of creating the table. Table Wizards provide an easy way to create common tables for business and personal use.

The following is a small sampling of the table structures for business use that you can choose from:

- Mailing List
- Employees
- Products
- Reservations

The following is a sampling of table structures for personal use that you can choose from:

- Household
- Inventory
- Recipes
- Plants
- Music Collection

2. Before showing you how to use the Table Wizard feature (later in this session), we'd like to lead you through creating a table structure from scratch. You will then have the understanding necessary to take advantage of all that the Table Wizard feature has to offer.
    CLICK: New Table
    The Table window should be displaying (Figure 2.2). Access is waiting for you to define the structure of the table in the grid. This view of the table is referred to as **Design view**. You will need to use Design view to define each Access object that you create; the Design view screen will look different depending on the object you are designing. A portion of the table structure that you'll be creating in this session, the Customers table, is pictured in Figure 2.3.

Figure 2.2

Access is waiting for you to define the structure of the table.

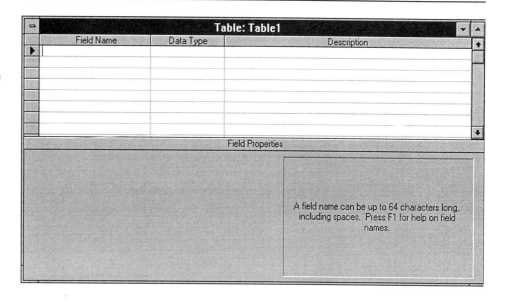

Figure 2.3

Partial structure for the Customers table

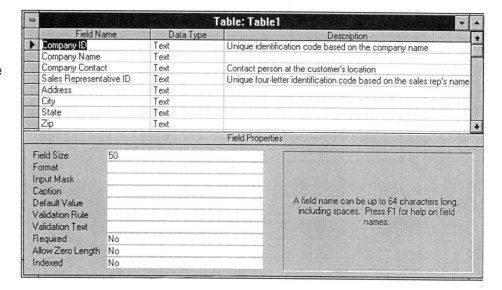

3. You must enter a unique name for each field in the table. Field names must start with a letter and, like all database objects, can be a maximum of 64 characters, including letters, numbers, spaces, and punctuation.

TYPE: Company ID
PRESS: [Tab] *to move to the Data Type column*
The cursor should now be positioned in the Data Type column.

Notice that Access automatically defined the Text data type. Also notice that the Field Properties box for the Customer ID field is now displaying in the bottom part of the table window (Figure 2.4) and that Access automatically set the Field Size to 50 characters. Fortunately, Access doesn't store the whole width of the field on disk, only the data you enter into the field. Therefore, it's fine to leave the width at 50 even if you're entering only a few characters in a field. (*Note*: We describe the the Field Properties box in more detail later when you modify the database structure.)

Figure 2.4

The Field Properties box for the Customer ID field is displaying

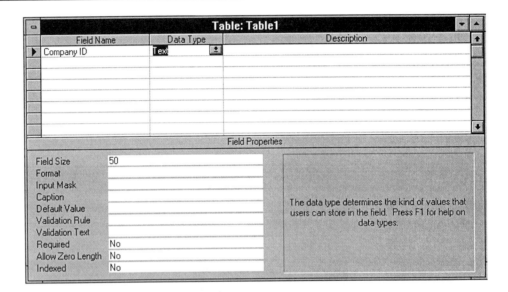

You must now select the type of data that the field will contain. Table 2.1 summarizes the available data types. The data type of each field in the Customer table, including the phone number and fax number fields, should be Text since you won't be performing calculations on any of these fields. Unless you choose a different data type, Access assumes the field data type is Text.

CAUTION: When creating table structures, it's important that you choose the correct data type before adding data records. You can change the data type after you've entered data; however, if the data types aren't compatible, you may lose data.

Table 2.1

Data Types

Type	Size in Characters	Stores
Text	Up to 255	Alphanumeric data, including letters, numbers, spaces, and punctuation symbols. Use this data type when the data doesn't need to be included in a calculation.
Memo	Up to 32,000	Alphanumeric data. Use this data type when you need to type several sentences or paragraphs to describe a record.
Number	1, 2, 4, or 8	Numeric data that can be used in calculations.
Date/Time	8	Dates and times.
Currency	8	Numbers with a leading dollar sign. Use this data type for currency values such as dollars, francs, or yen.
Counter	4	A numeric value that Access automatically increments for each record you add to a table.
Yes/No	1 bit (8 bits make up a character)	Logical or boolean values. Use this field for yes/no or true/false data.
OLE Object	Up to a gigabyte (limited by disk space)	OLE (Object Linking and Embedding) objects, graphics, or other binary data

4. Even though you don't need to change the data type for the Customer ID field, we want to show you how to change the column type.
CLICK: ⬇ *in the Data Type field*
CLICK: Number
Note that "Number" is now displaying in the Data Type column and that different properties are displaying in the Field Properties area. To change the type back to Text:
CLICK: ⬇ *in the Data Type field*
CLICK: Text

5. To move the cursor into the Description column:
    PRESS: ⌷Tab⌷

6. A short description of each field helps you to remember the purpose of
    the field; it's optional whether you enter data into this field. The
    description displays on the status line when you select the field in a
    form (forms are described in more detail in this session and in
    Session 5).
    TYPE: Unique identification code based on the
        company name
    PRESS: ⌷Tab⌷
    Access is now waiting for you to define the second field in the table.

7. Refer to the following information to complete the structure for the
    Customer table:

Field Name	*Data Type*	*Description (Optional)*
Company Name	Text	
Company Contact	Text	Contact person at the customer's location
Sales Representative ID	Text	Unique four-letter identification code based on the sales rep's name
Address	Text	
City	Text	
State	Text	
Zip	Text	
Phone	Text	Direct phone line to contact person at customer location
Fax	Text	Fax line to contact person at customer location

    (*Note*: To make a change in any of the fields in the table structure, point to
    the field and then click. Then make your changes.)

8. Move on to the next section. You will learn about primary keys,
    indexes, and saving the table structure you just completed.

SETTING A PRIMARY KEY

If you try to save the Customer table right now, Access will indicate that
you haven't yet defined a **primary key**, which is a field in the table that
uniquely identifies each record. A primary key is used by Access to more

easily search for and find data stored in data tables, and to define relationships between tables. For these reasons, it is highly recommended that you define a primary key, even though it isn't required. Once a primary key is defined for a table, the table's datasheet is automatically indexed, or sorted, into order by the primary key.

Keep the following in mind when working with primary keys:

- The primary key is the main index for the data table and the datasheet is displayed in order by the primary key. For example, if you define the Lastname field as the primary key, the datasheet will display in order by the Lastname field.

- If two records have the same data in the primary key field, Access will generate an error message. You must either get rid of the duplicate values, define a different primary key, or include an additional field in the primary key.

- A primary key can be based on one field or on multiple fields. An example of a multiple-field primary key is one that is based on the Lastname field and the Firstname field. Those records that have the same Lastname will be put into order by the Firstname field.

To set a primary key, select the field you want to sort by and then click the primary key button (🔑), or choose Edit, Set Primary Key from the Menu bar. To set a multiple-field primary key, hold down Ctrl and click the field selector to the left of each field that you want to include in the primary key. Then click 🔑, or choose Edit, Set Primary Key from the Menu bar.

For now, we're going to lead you through defining the Company ID field as the primary key field. (*Note*: If you don't specify a primary key, Access can define one for you by creating an ID field that contains the Counter data type. This simple primary key works for most tasks.)

1. The Field Properties data is now displaying in the bottom left of the Table window.
   SELECT: Company ID row *by clicking in the field selector area to the left of the field name*
   CHOOSE: Edit, Set Primary Key
   A key should now be displaying to the left of the Company ID field name. Also, notice that "Yes (No Duplicates)" is displaying opposite the Indexed option in the Field Properties area; this makes sense since duplicate field data isn't allowed in primary key fields.

Quick Reference *Setting a Primary* *Key*	While viewing the table structure in Design view, select the appropriate field row, and then choose Edit, Set Primary Key from the menu or click [🔑] in the Button bar.

2. Now that you've defined the structure for the Customer table and have set a primary key, you must save the Customer table. By doing so, the Customer table structure is saved as part of the SPORTING.MDB file. After you save the Customer table, "Customer" will display in the Database window.
   CHOOSE: File, Save
   TYPE: Customer
   PRESS: [Enter] or CLICK: OK

3. To display the Database window:
   CHOOSE: File, Close
   (Or double-click the Control menu (▭) in the upper-left corner of the table window.)

4. The Database window should be displaying.

To remove a primary key, you must choose View, Indexes from the Menu bar, or click the Indexes button (📝); this procedure is described in the next section.

Quick Reference
Defining a Table
Structure
	1. CLICK: Table button *in the Database window*
	2. SELECT: New *in the Database window*
	3. Type in a field name and then press [Tab] to move to the Data Type column.
	4. SELECT: a data type
	   PRESS: [Tab] *to move to the Description column*
	5. TYPE: a description *(optional)*
	   PRESS: [Tab] *to begin defining the second field*
	6. Continue with steps 3–5 until all fields have been defined.
	7. SELECT: a primary key (optional)
	   Access can create one for you if you don't specify one yourself.
	8. Save the structure by choosing File, Save from the Menu bar.

DEFINING AND REMOVING INDEXES

In addition to a primary key, Access lets you create indexes to be used with your data tables. An **index** is stored with the table and contains pointers that determine the order of table records. You should create an index for a field if you anticipate often searching for or sorting data that is based on that field. (*Note*: You learn how to perform searches in Session 3.)

When records are added to a table that has a primary key or has been indexed into order, the primary key and indexes are automatically updated. For this reason, indexes can slow down data entry. Depending on the size of a table, an index might not speed up your searches very much. If your searches and sorting tasks are performed fast enough, maybe you don't need to create indexes.

In this section we lead you through creating an index for the Customer table and then deleting the index. (*Note*: To delete a primary key, use the same procedure as for deleting an index.)

1. The Database window should be displaying. To create an index, you must first display the table structure.
   CLICK: Customer table name
   CLICK: <u>D</u>esign button *in the Database window*
   The Customer table structure is displaying.

2. To create an index for the City field:
   CLICK: field selection area to the left of the City field name

3. Use the Field Properties area to create an index.
   CLICK: Indexed
   CLICK: ⬇
   The following indexing options are displaying. (*Note*: You learn more about Field Properties later in this session.)

Table 2.2	*Indexed Property Setting*	*Description*
Indexing Options	No	Don't create an index on this field. Also, use this option to delete a previously created index.
	Yes (Duplicates OK)	Create an index on this field; fields can contain the same data. For example, a City field should be indexed using this option since more than one record will likely pertain to the same city.
	Yes (No Duplicates)	Create an index on this field; like primary key fields, no two fields can contain the same data. (For example, you may want a Part Numbers field to be indexed with this option, since no two part numbers are the same.)

4. SELECT: Yes (Duplicates OK)

5. To view the indexes you have defined:
   CHOOSE: <u>V</u>iew, <u>I</u>ndexes, or

   CLICK: ![button] button

   The following window, which displays a list of the current indexes, should be displaying:

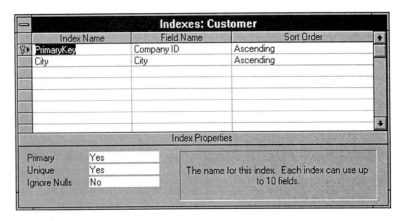

6. To delete the City index:
   SELECT: *the City row in the Indexes window*
   PRESS: [Delete]
   (*Note*: You could have removed the index by setting the field property to "No".)

7. To close the Indexes window:
   DOUBLE-CLICK: Indexes Control menu (━)

8. To display the Database window:
   CHOOSE: File, Close
   (Or double-click the Control menu (━) in the upper-left corner of the
   Table window.)

9. Since you made changes to the table structure:
   CLICK: Yes *in response to the prompt*
   The Database window should be displaying.

Quick Reference *Defining an Index*	1. In Design view, select the field you want to work with. 2. In the Field Properties area: CLICK: Indexed CLICK: [⬇] Select an indexing option.

Quick Reference *Removing an Index*	Remove an index using one of the following methods: 1. In Design view, select the field you want to work with. 2. In the Field Properties area: CLICK: Indexed CLICK: [⬇] SELECT: No *or* 1. In Design view: CHOOSE: View, Indexes 2. In the Indexes window: SELECT: *the field row you want to delete* PRESS: [Delete]

Quick Reference *Removing a* *Primary Key*	1. In Design view: CHOOSE: View, Indexes 2. In the Indexes window: SELECT: *the field row that contains the primary key* PRESS: [Delete]

ADDING RECORDS

In this section you will display the Customer table (stored in the SPORTING database) and then add a few records. You will enter the records while displaying the table's datasheet. Then, you learn how to create a form and use it to enter the rest of the Customer data.

At this point, the Database window should be displaying with the Customer table name. Perform the following steps to add three records to the Customer table:

1. To display the datasheet for the Customer table, use one of the following procedures:

    DOUBLE-CLICK: the Customer table name, or

    SELECT: the Customer table name
    CLICK: <u>O</u>pen button in the Database window
    The Customer datasheet should be displaying on the screen (Figure 2.5). The cursor is positioned in the Company ID field and the field description (that you typed when creating the table structure) is displaying on the Status bar.

Figure 2.5

The Customer datasheet is displaying on the screen. At this point, the datasheet is empty.

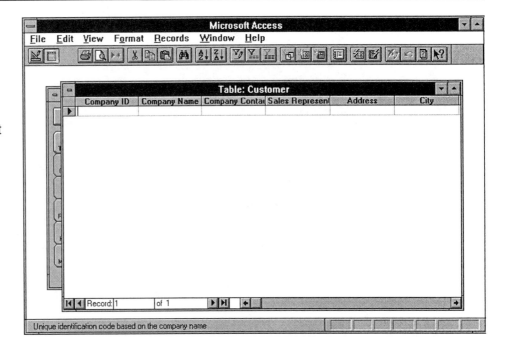

2. After typing data into a field, press `Tab` to move to the next field. You will notice that some data is too wide to display in the column. You learn how to widen columns later in this session. For now, let the text scroll in the field window.

   TYPE: ROSI

   (*Note*: The code "ROSI" is derived from the first four letters of the company name, which you will type in next.)

   PRESS: `Tab`

   The cursor is now positioned in the Company Name field.

   TYPE: Rosie's Cookie Company

   PRESS: `Tab`

   TYPE: Jean Arston

   PRESS: `Tab`

   TYPE: VTRI

   PRESS: `Tab`

   TYPE: 90 Spruce Street

   PRESS: `Tab`

   TYPE: San Mateo

   PRESS: `Tab`

   TYPE: CA

   PRESS: `Tab`

   TYPE: 94010

   PRESS: `Tab`

   TYPE: 415-555-5550

   PRESS: `Tab`

   TYPE: 415-555-5551

   PRESS: `Tab` *so you can begin typing the second record*

The cursor should have moved to the first field in the second record. When the cursor left the first record, the first record was automatically saved onto the disk. You don't need to do anything else to save the data. Also, while entering a record, Access put a pencil symbol to the left of the record you're working on. As described earlier, this pencil is called the **record indicator** and is displayed when you've made changes to the current record, but haven't saved the changes. If the cursor is in a record that has been changed, the record indicator looks like a right-pointing triangle. Once you start typing into this record, an asterisk will display one record below, which marks the empty record at the bottom of the table.

3. Refer to the following to enter data into the next two records:

Record 2	*Record 3*
ABCM	SILV
ABC Metals	Silver Spring Toyota
Frances Hillman	Steve Yap
PVIE	RHEU
550 Montgomery Street	223 Main Street
San Francisco	Sacramento
CA	CA
94104	95825
415-999-9990	916-888-8880
415-999-9991	916-888-8881

The Table window should look similar to Figure 2.6.

Figure 2.6

The Customer datasheet after three records have been entered. Notice that the records contain too many fields to fit on the screen at once. Also, in a few cases, the columns need to be widened.

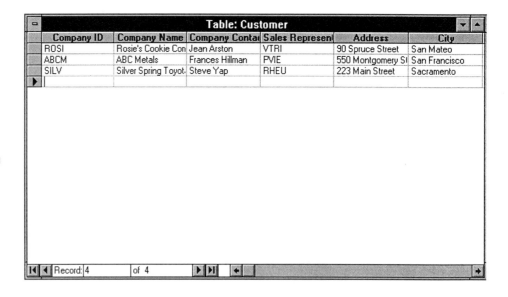

After you enter data into a datasheet, you can move the cursor and edit data using one or more of the shortcuts in Table 2.3. You can also view fields that aren't currently in view by dragging the thumb on the horizontal scroll bar in the desired direction.

4. Practice moving the thumb on the scroll bar and using some of the techniques described in Table 2.3.

Table 2.3

Datasheet Editing
Techniques

Procedure	*Description*
Tab	Move to the next field in a record
Shift + Tab	Move to the previous field in a record
Home , End	Move to first or last field in a record
F2	Select/deselect the current field
Esc	Undo changes you've made to the current field or record
Ctrl + "	Replace the value in a field with the value of the same field in the previous record

5. Notice that the records aren't displaying in order by the primary key, the Company ID field. If you leave the datasheet and then redisplay the datasheet, the records will display in order by the primary key. To illustrate:
    CHOOSE: View, Table Design
    CLICK: View, Datasheet
    Note that the records are now displaying in order by the Company ID field.

6. Close the Table window so that the Database window displays. Use one of the following two procedures:

    CHOOSE: File, Close, *or*
    DOUBLE-CLICK: the Control menu (◪) in the upper-left corner of the table window

7. The Database window should be displaying.

In the next section, we lead you through creating a form and then adding the remaining records to the Customer table.

CREATING A FORM WITH THE AUTOFORM WIZARD

When you create a data table, the data in the table is automatically displayed in a datasheet; that is, in rows and columns. In Datasheet view, you can see more than one record and field on the screen. There may be times when you want to see only one record on the screen at once so that you can view or edit it. You can do this by creating a **form**, which is simply a screen design through which you can look at and modify data stored in a table. Many people find it easier to view table data in **Form view** rather than in Datasheet view.

In this section we lead you through creating the form using the **AutoForm Wizard**, which automatically creates a form for you without asking you any questions. The form includes all the fields in the selected table. In Session 5, you learn how to customize a form.

Perform the following steps:

1. The SPORTING Database window should be displaying on the screen. If it isn't:
    CLICK: 🗁
    SELECT: *the drive that contains the Adantage Diskette in the Drives text box*
    SELECT: SPORTING.MDB
    PRESS: Enter or CLICK: OK

2. To create a form for the Customer table:
    SELECT: Customer table name
    (*Note*: It may already be selected.)

3. To create a form:
    CLICK: AutoForm button (🗐) in the Tool bar

4. You might not be able to see the entire record on the screen. To maximize the Form window so you can see all the records:
    CLICK: Maximize button (▲) *in the Form window*
    The Form window should look like Figure 2.7.

Figure 2.7

This form was
created with the
AutoForm Wizard
for use with the
Customer table.
The Form window
has been
maximized.

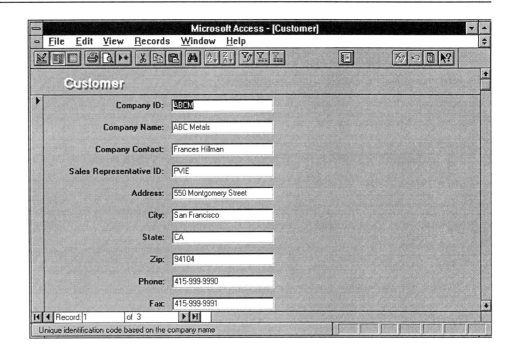

5. Before continuing, save the form specifications:
   CHOOSE: File, Save Form *from the Menu bar*
   TYPE: Sporting, Inc Customers
   (*Note*: Access doesn't allow you to use a period (.) when naming objects.)

Quick Reference *Using the AutoForm Wizard*	1. Display the Database window. SELECT: *a table name*
	2. CLICK: AutoForm button (🔲)
	3. If necessary, after the form displays, click the Maximize button (▲) to see the entire window.

While displaying the form, to move from record to record use the buttons
on the bottom-left of the Form window. We describe these buttons in
Table 2.4. *Note*: You can both view and edit the records in a table while it
is in Form view.

Table 2.4	Button	Description
Form Window Buttons	⏮	Display the first record in the table
	◀	Display the previous record in the table
	▶	Display the next record in the table
	⏭	Display the last record in the table

1. To go to the first blank record in the database so that you can add more Customer data:
   CLICK: ⏭ *to display the last record in the table*
   CLICK: ▶ *to display the next blank record*

2. Type in the data pictured below. Like when entering data in Datasheet view, press [Tab] and [Shift]+[Tab] to move from field to field.

Company ID	Company Name	Company Contact	Sales Repre	Address	City	State	Zip	Phone	Fax
BREW	Brewery Supplies, Inc.	Randy Brewski	PVIE	9999 River Forest Drive	Houston	TX	77079	713-666-6660	713-666-6661
COMP	Computers, Intl.	Cecilia Adams	KCLI	7771 Shannon Square	Clackamas	Oregon	97015	503-222-2222	503-222-2221
DISC	Discount Glass	Moira Walsh	KAND	2222 50th Street	Northfield	IL	60093	708-333-3331	708-333-3332
FARM	Farming Equipment, Inc	Bruce Towne	JAZA	14499 3rd Avenue	Walnut Grove	CA	95690	916-776-1332	916-776-1333
FLOW	Flowers Anywhere	Kela Henderson	JAZA	80 Rockford Square	Bushland	TX	79012	806-111-1111	806-111-1112
NATI	National Dentistry	Camilla Edsell	RHEU	101 6th Street, SE	Phoenix	Arizona	05021	602-444-4441	602-444-4442
PAPE	Paper Supplies, Etc.	Tessa Huberty	VTRI	111 Glen Vista	Ventura	CA	93003	805-111-1111	805-111-1112
PUBL	Publishing Etc.	Rich Williams	KAND	2000 Hilltop Way	Incline Village	NV	89450	702-111-1111	702-111-1112
SCHU	Schuler and Co.	Presley Schuler, Jr.	KCLI	1000 Tower Plaza	Stockton	CA	95204	209-777-7771	209-777-7772

3. When you're finished typing in all the Customer data, make sure to press [Tab] to move the cursor to a blank record so that the previous record is saved. (Remember that a record is saved once you move to a new record.)

4. To display the data in a datasheet, use the Datasheet view button (▦) that's displaying on the Tool bar.
   CLICK: ▦

5. To display the data in a form, use the Form view button (▤):
   CLICK: ▤
   Practice switching between the two view modes.

6. To close the current window so that the Database window displays:
   CHOOSE: File, Close

7. Notice that the Database window is maximized as a result of maximizing the Form window earlier. To reduce the size of the Database window:

   CLICK: Restore button (⬍) *in the top-right corner of the Database window*

The Database window should be displaying in its default size.

Quick Reference *Switching Between Datasheet and Form View*	• When displaying a form, to switch to Datasheet view, click 🖩, located on the Tool bar. • When displaying a datasheet, to switch to Form view, click 🖩, located on the Tool bar.

In the next section, we lead you through customizing the Datasheet view of the Customer table.

CUSTOMIZING THE DATASHEET VIEW

There are numerous options for customizing the appearance, or layout, of a datasheet. Because a datasheet is an image of the underlying table data, you can manipulate the datasheet's column widths, row height, and field order without affecting the table structure itself. The changes that you make to the datasheet are only available for the current work session, unless you choose File, Save Layout from the Menu bar. After saving, Access will display the table in this layout the next time you view the datasheet.

ADJUSTING THE COLUMN WIDTHS

In Datasheet view, to change the width of a column, you point to the column border between the field names at the top of the table, and then drag the border in the desired direction. Or choose Layout, Column Width from the Menu bar and type in the desired column width.

Perform the following steps:

1. The SPORTING Database window should be displaying on the screen. If it isn't:
    CLICK: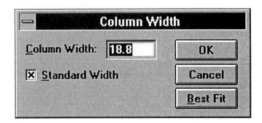
    SELECT: *the drive that contains the Adantage Diskette in the Drives text box*
    SELECT: SPORTING.MDB
    PRESS: [Enter] or CLICK: OK

2. To display the Customer datasheet:
    DOUBLE-CLICK: Customer table name

3. If the datasheet isn't displaying in full size, click the Maximize button (▲) in the Table window.

4. Position the pointer between the Company Name and Company Contact field names. Notice that the mouse pointer changed to a vertical bar with an arrow through it.

5. Drag the column border to the right until you can see all the text in the Company Name column.

6. On your own, widen the Company Contact and Address fields.

You can also use the Menu bar to change column widths. In the next step you will widen the Sales Representative ID field.

1. Position the cursor in the Sales Representative ID field.

2. CHOOSE: Format, Column Width
    The following dialog box should be displaying:

3. To widen the column so that the column is wide enough to display the column heading and data:
    CLICK: Best Fit button

4. Keep the datasheet on the screen. You will adjust row heights in the next section.

Quick Reference *Adjusting Column Widths in a Datasheet*	1. Position the pointer between two field names until the mouse pointer changes to a vertical bar with an arrow through it. 2. Drag the column border to the right or left until the column is the desired width. *or* 1. Position the cursor in the column you want to widen. 2. CHOOSE: Format, Column Width 3. Type in a new column width and press (Enter) or click the Best Fit button.

ADJUSTING ROW HEIGHTS

By default, the current font determines the row height. Row height is measured in **points**, which are a typographical measurement equal to 1/72 inch. In Datasheet view, to change the height of all rows in a datasheet, you point to any border between two rows to the left of the first field column, and then drag the border up or down. Or choose Format, Row Height from the Menu bar and type in the desired height.

Perform the following steps:

1. To change the row height using the Menu bar:
   CHOOSE: Format, Row Height
   The following dialog box displays:

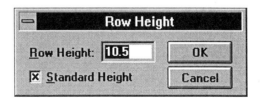

Note that a check appears in the Standard Height box. When this is checked, the row height conforms to the current font selection. Once you type in a new point size, the check mark disappears.

2. To change the height to 14 points:
   TYPE: 14
   PRESS: (Enter) or CLICK: OK
   All the rows in the Customer datasheet are now larger.

3. To change the row height back to its original setting:
   CHOOSE: Format, Row Height
   CLICK: Standard Height check box
   PRESS: [Enter] or CLICK: OK

4. Keep the datasheet on the screen. You will change the displayed font
   in the next section.

Quick Reference *Adjusting Row* *Heights in a* *Datasheet*	CHOOSE: Format, Row Height TYPE: *a row height* PRESS: [Enter] or CLICK: OK *or* Point to any border between two rows to the left of the first field column, and then drag the border up or down.

CHANGING THE DISPLAYED FONT

By default, Access displays table data using an 8 point MS Sans Serif font.
You can change the font characteristics of table data by choosing Format,
Font from the Menu bar. As for row height, the entire datasheet is affected.
Once you choose Format, Font, the following dialog box displays:

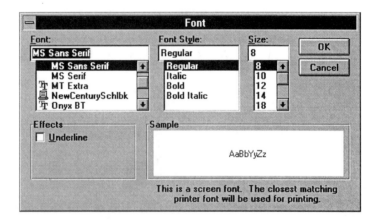

Perform the following steps:

1. To change the font from MS Sans Serif to MS Serif:
   CHOOSE: Format, Font
   CLICK: MS Serif *in Font list box*
   Notice that the Sample box changes to reflect your selections.

2. To change the size to 12 points:
   CLICK: 12 *in the Size list box*
   PRESS: (Enter) or CLICK: OK
   The datasheet should look similar to Figure 2.8. Notice that the columns aren't wide enough to display the newly selected font.

Figure 2.8

The font has been changed to MS Serif, 12 point.

	Company ID	Company Name	Company Conta	Sales Representativ	Address	
▶	ABCM	ABC Metals	Frances Hillman	PVIE	550 Montgomery St	San
	BREW	Brewery Supplies, I	Randy Brewski	PVIE	9999 River Forest D	Hou:
	COMP	Computers, Intl.	Cecilia Adams	KCLI	7771 Shannon Squar	Clac
	DISC	Discount Glass	Moira Walsh	KAND	2222 50th Street	Nort
	FARM	Farming Equipment	Bruce Towne	JAZA	14499 3rd Avenue	Walr
	FLOW	Flowers Anywhere	Kela Henderson	JAZA	80 Rockford Square	Bush
	NATI	National Dentistry	Camilla Edsell	RHEU	101 6th Street, SE	Phoe
	PAPE	Paper Supplies, Etc.	Tessa Huberty	VTRI	111 Glen Vista	Vent
	PUBL	Publishing Etc.	Rich Williams	KAND	2000 Hilltop Way	Inclii
	ROSI	Rosie's Cookie Com	Jean Arston	VTRI	90 Spruce Street	San
	SCHU	Schuler and Co.	Presley Schuler, J	KCLI	1000 Tower Plaza	Stocl
	SILV	Silver Spring Toyoti	Steve Yap	RHEU	223 Main Street	Sacri
*						

3. To change the font back to what it was originally:
   CHOOSE: Format, Font
   CLICK: MS Sans Serif *in Font list box (you may need to click the up arrow once to view the MS Sans Serif font)*
   CLICK: 8 *in the Size list box (you may need to drag the vertical scroll bar upwards)*
   PRESS: (Enter) or CLICK: OK

Quick Reference	CHOOSE: Format, Font
Changing the	SELECT: a font *in the Font list box*
Displayed Font	SELECT: a size *in the Size list box*
	PRESS: (Enter) or CLICK: OK

REORDERING FIELDS

In Datasheet view, field columns are displayed in the same order in which they appear in the table structure. For a different view of your data, you can move the columns in a datasheet. To move a column, you must select it and then drag it to a new location. In this section you will move the Company Contact field so that it displays before the Company Name field.

Perform the following steps:

1. To select the Company Contact column, point to the Company Contact field name. A downward-pointing arrow should be displaying. Click with the mouse. The entire column should be selected.

2. To move the column to the left, click the field name again and then drag the column to the left, over the Company Name field. When the pointer is where you want to position the column, release the mouse button. The columns should be reordered (Figure 2.9).

Figure 2.9

The fields in the Customer datasheet have been reordered.

Company ID	Company Contact	Company Name	Sales Representative ID	Address	
ABCM	Frances Hillman	ABC Metals	PVIE	550 Montgomery Street	San Fra
BREW	Randy Brewski	Brewery Supplies, Inc.	PVIE	9999 River Forest Drive	Housto
COMP	Cecilia Adams	Computers, Intl.	KCLI	7771 Shannon Square	Clacka
DISC	Moira Walsh	Discount Glass	KAND	2222 50th Street	Northfie
FARM	Bruce Towne	Farming Equipment, Inc.	JAZA	14499 3rd Avenue	Walnut
FLOW	Kela Henderson	Flowers Anywhere	JAZA	80 Rockford Square	Bushla
NATI	Camilla Edsell	National Dentistry	RHEU	101 6th Street, SE	Phoeni
PAPE	Tessa Huberty	Paper Supplies, Etc.	VTRI	111 Glen Vista	Ventura
PUBL	Rich Williams	Publishing Etc.	KAND	2000 Hilltop Way	Incline
ROSI	Jean Arston	Rosie's Cookie Company	VTRI	90 Spruce Street	San Ma
SCHU	Presley Schuler, Jr.	Schuler and Co.	KCLI	1000 Tower Plaza	Stockt
SILV	Steve Yap	Silver Spring Toyota	RHEU	223 Main Street	Sacram

Quick Reference
Moving a Field

1. Select the column (field) that you want to move by pointing to the field name and then clicking. The entire column should be selected.
2. To move the column, click the field name again and then drag the column in the desired direction (left or right). When the column is in the correct location, release the mouse button.

SAVING THE DATASHEET LAYOUT

In this section, we don't want you to save the datasheet layout, but we'd like to describe how to perform the save procedure. All of the changes you made in the previous sections are temporary; that is, once you close the Table window, Access forgets your layout specifications. To save your layout specifications so they can be used in a future work session, you would choose File, Save Layout from the Menu bar.

Since we *don't* want you to save the changed layout:

1. CHOOSE: File, Close

2. Since you don't want to save the layout changes:
    SELECT: No
    The Database window should be displaying.

Quick Reference *Saving the Datasheet Layout*	CHOOSE: File, Save Layout *from the menu*

MODIFYING THE TABLE STRUCTURE

After working with a data table, you may find that you need an additional field or that one of the existing fields needs to be wider. Modifying a structure in Microsoft Access is as simple as editing a table. By clicking the Design button in the Database window, you can add fields, delete fields, and modify data types in a structure. However, you should not perform structural changes carelessly. When you modify a table's structure, you also modify the forms and reports that are based on the table.

INSERTING AND DELETING FIELDS

In the Database window, after highlighting the table name that you want to work with, click the Design button to display the table's structure. To insert a row, position the cursor in the row where a new row (which corresponds to a field in the table) should be inserted, and then choose Edit, Insert Row from the Menu bar. To delete a row, position the cursor in the row that you want to delete, and then choose Edit, Delete Row.

Perform the following steps:

1. The SPORTING Database window should be displaying on the screen. If it isn't:
   CLICK: 📂
   SELECT: *the drive that contains the Advantage Diskette in the Drives text box*
   SELECT: SPORTING.MDB
   PRESS: [Enter] or CLICK: OK

2. To modify the structure of the Customers table:
   SELECT: the Customer table name
   CLICK: Design
   The structure of the Customer table should be displaying on the screen.

3. To insert a new field beneath the Company ID field, you position the cursor on the Company Name field (second row):
   PRESS: [↓]

4. To insert a Company Size field:
   CHOOSE: Edit, Insert Row
   TYPE: Company Size
   PRESS: [Tab]
   CLICK: [±] *in the Data Type field*
   SELECT: Number
   PRESS: [Tab]
   TYPE: Number of employees

5. To save the Customer table:
   CHOOSE: File, Save

6. To view the Customer datasheet:
   CHOOSE: View, Datasheet, or
   CLICK: Datasheet icon (▦)
   Notice that the Company Size field is now displaying in the Customer datasheet.

7. To enter Design view again so you can delete the Company Size field:
   CHOOSE: View, Table Design, or
   CLICK: Design icon (▧)

8. Position the cursor in the Company Size field.

9. CHOOSE: Edit, Delete Row
   CLICK: OK
   The Company Size field is no longer displaying in the structure.

10. To save the Customer table:
    CHOOSE: File, Save

11. To view the Customer datasheet:
    CHOOSE: View, Datasheet, or

    CLICK: Datasheet icon (▦)
    Notice that the Company Size field is no longer displaying.

Quick Reference	

Quick Reference
Inserting and
Deleting Fields in a
Table Structure
	1. In the Database window, select the table you want to work with and then click Design.
	2. Press ⬇ until the cursor is positioned where you want to insert/delete a field.
	3. CHOOSE: Edit, Insert Row, or
	   CHOOSE: Edit, Delete Row
	4. When finished:
	   CHOOSE: File, Save

SETTING FIELD PROPERTIES

In this section we describe the process of setting field properties. Every field in a table has a set of properties. By defining a field's properties, you take control of how table data is stored and displayed. With Access, you can define the following properties for each field:

- Field Size   With this property you can define the maximum length of a text or numeric field. Use this option if you know that all of the entries in a particular field are less than a certain number.

- Format   Use this property to specify how numbers are displayed. For example, you can display numbers with a leading dollar sign or dates in a specific format.

- Decimal Places   For numeric fields, use this property to specify the number of places to display to the right of the decimal.

- Input Mask

    To simplify data entry for fields that have the same format, such as phone number fields, create an input mask. For example, the input mask for a phone field might look like: (415)___-____.

- Caption

    Use this property to define a default field label.

- Default Value

    Use this option to enter a value or expression that is automatically entered when fields are created. For example, if the most of the numbers in a Phone field begin with 555, type 555- in as the Default Value expression.

- Validation Rule

    Use this option to enter an expression that defines the rules for entering data into a specific field. For example, if you specify the Validation Rule of ">3" in a restaurant's Reservation field, Access will display an error message if you attempt to type 1, 2, or 3 into the field.

- Validation Text

    Use this option to define the text that displays if you enter invalid data into a field. For example, in the Validation Rule example above, the text "We only accept reservations for 4 or more people" might display when the user types a number that is less than 4.

- Required

    Use this option to specify whether a value is required in a field. If a value is required, Access displays an error message if you attempt to skip entering data into the field.

- Allow Zero Length

    By default, Access stores a null value in an empty field. To store a zero-length string of text, type " " into the field after changing the Allow Zero Length field property to Yes. Zero length strings behave differently than null values. For example, if a query is based on a field with a null value, the record isn't included in the resulting dynaset.

- Indexed   Use this field to specify whether the table should be indexed on this field in order to speed searches.

The steps for setting a field property are:

1. In Design view, select the field whose properties you want to set.

2. Click the appropriate property in the bottom of the Design view window.

3. Set the property.

4. Save the new structure specifications by choosing File, Save from the Menu bar.

Quick Reference *Setting Field* *Properties*	1. While viewing the database structure (in Design view), select the field whose properties you want to set. 2. Click the appropriate property in the bottom of the Design view window. 3. Set the property. 4. To save the file structure: CHOOSE: File, Save

PRINTING A TABLE

Now that you've created a table, you probably want to know how to print it. You can either print the datasheet or the table definition. The **table definition** is a listing of the structure of the data table. The table definition printout is useful if you want to refer to it while creating the structure of a related table.

PRINTING THE DATASHEET

To print a datasheet, choose File, Print from the Menu bar. The following dialog box will display:

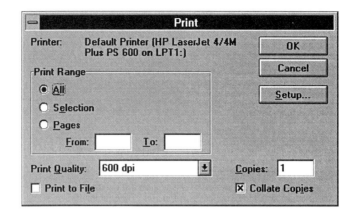

Access prints a datasheet as it appears on the screen. For datasheets that are too large to print on a sheet of paper, Access prints them from left to right and then from top to bottom. For example, if your datasheet is four pages wide and two pages long, Access prints the top four pages first and then the bottom four pages. To print a datasheet in Landscape mode (across the length of the paper), which is often used for printing wide datasheets, select Setup and then click the Landscape button (located in the Orientation area). Then press (Enter) or click OK to display the Print dialog box (shown above).

Perform the following steps to print the Customer table:

1. Make sure the Customer datasheet is displaying on the screen.

2. To print:
    CHOOSE: File, Print
    (*Note*: To print in Landscape mode, select Setup and then click the Landscape button. Then press (Enter) or click OK.)

3. To print the entire datasheet:
    PRESS: (Enter) or CLICK: OK
    The Customer table should be printing.

4   To close the current window so that the Database window displays:
    CHOOSE: File, Close

You don't have to always print *every* record in a datasheet. If you select a group of records before choosing File, Print, choose the Selection option to print the selected records. (*Note*: In Session 3, you learn how to create queries which you use to list the records that meet your criteria. Once this dynaset is listed on the screen, you can print the dynaset using the procedures described in this section.)

Quick Reference	1. CHOOSE: File, Print
Printing a Table	2. If necessary, select Setup and then click Landscape. Then press (Enter) or click OK. 3. To print the entire datasheet: PRESS: (Enter) or CLICK: OK

PRINTING THE TABLE DEFINITION

To print the table definition, or table structure, perform the following steps:

1. The SPORTING Database window should be displaying.

2. SELECT: Customer table name

3. CHOOSE: File, Print Definition
   The following Print Table Definition dialog box should be displaying:

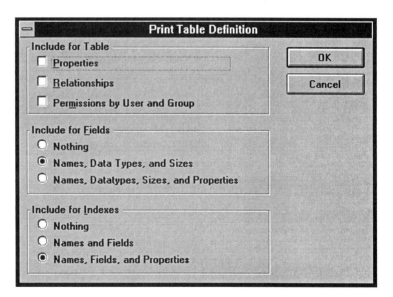

(*Note*: Option selections may be different on your computer.)

4. To print the basic structure (without detailed properties information):
   CLICK: Names, Data Types, and Sizes
   CLICK: Names, Fields, and Properties
   PRESS: (Enter) or CLICK: OK

5. A partial preview of the structure should be displaying on the screen. To print the structure:
CHOOSE: File, Print
PRESS: (Enter) or CLICK: OK
(*Note*: You may have to wait a few seconds for the printout to be generated.)

Quick Reference	1. CHOOSE: File, Print Definition
Printing a Table	2. If necessary, make selections in the Print Table Definition dialog
Definition	box.
	3. To print the definition:
	CHOOSE: File, Print
	PRESS: (Enter) or CLICK: OK

USING THE TABLE WIZARD

Now that you've gone through the process of creating a table structure from scratch and modifying it, it is time to show you how to use Access's Table Wizard feature to simplify the process of creating a table structure. The Table Wizard feature provides you with sample table structures from which you can build your own tables. For example, one table structure, Recipes, contains 15 fields from which you can choose to build your own Recipe table. You can either include all the fields or be selective about which fields to include in the new table.

In this section, we lead you through using the Table Wizard to create a simple table structure to store recipes. You will then delete the Recipe table object from the disk. Perform the following steps:

1. The SPORTING Database window should be displaying.
CLICK: Table button
CLICK: New button
CLICK: Table Wizards
The Table Wizard dialog box is displaying (see below):

Notice that "Business" is chosen in the bottom-left corner of the Table Wizard dialog box. As a result, sample business-related table structures are listing in the Sample Tables list box.

2. To see a listing of some "Personal" tables:
   CLICK: Personal button
   Notice that different table names are now displaying in the Sample Tables list box.

3. Since the Friends table name is currently selected, a list of corresponding fields is listing in the Sample Fields list box.
   CLICK: Guests table name
   Notice that different field names are now listing in the Sample Fields list box.

4. To create a table structure that stores recipes:
   CLICK: Recipes table name

5. To include all the Recipes fields on the form:
   CLICK: the >> button
   (*Note*: The > button selects only one field at a time.)

6. CLICK: Finish button
   After a few seconds, the Recipes datasheet should be displaying.

7. To see what Access did for you automatically:
   CLICK: Design View button(⟰)

8. To display the Database window:
    DOUBLE-CLICK: the Control menu (◘) in the upper-left corner of the
        window

The Recipes table name should now be listing in the Database window. It's
that easy! Access can save you a lot of time if you're creating a table
structure that can be based on one of Access's Business or Personal table
templates.

In the following steps, you will delete the Recipes table:

1. SELECT: Recipes table name

2. CHOOSE: Edit, Delete, or
    PRESS: (Delete)
    CLICK: OK

3. The Database window is now displaying. To close this window using
    the Database Control menu:

    DOUBLE-CLICK: ◘ *in the upper-left corner of the window*
    The Microsoft Access workspace looks as it did when you first loaded
    the program.

SUMMARY

In this session, you learned how to create the structure for a database and
add data to a table while displaying it in Datasheet view. You also created
a form using an AutoForm Wizard and then added some additional data to
the table. When creating a structure, you must enter a unique field name
and select a data type for each storage field in the table. Although you can
later modify its structure, it is important that you have a good
understanding of a data table's purpose and how it fits into the database
before creating it. Several steps were outlined in this session to help you
plan and design your databases.

You learned how to customize the presentation of data from a table. You
altered column widths and row heights, and reordered fields. You also
learned how to modify a database structure and about using field
properties.

COMMAND SUMMARY

Table 2.5 provides a summary of the commands introduced in this session.

Table 2.5	*COMMAND*	*TASK*
Command Summary	File, New Database	Create a new database
	In Design view, select the appropriate field row, and then choose Edit, Set Primary Key from the menu.	Set a primary key
	Click Table button in the Database window, New	Define a table structure
	Select a table name, click [icon]	Use the AutoForm Wizard to create a form
	Click [icon] to switch to Datasheet view. Click [icon] to switch to Form view.	Switch between Datasheet and Form view
	Position the pointer between two field names and drag the column border to the left or right.	Adjust column widths in a datasheet
	Format, Column Width	Adjust column widths
	Format, Row Height	Adjust row heights in a datasheet
	Layout, Font	Change the displayed font
	Select the column and then drag the column to the desired location.	Move a field (column) in a datasheet
	File, Save Layout	Save the datasheet layout

Display the table in Design view, Edit, Insert Row (or Edit, Delete Row)	Insert/delete fields in a table structure
File, Print Definition	Print a table's definition, or structure.
File, Print	Print a table

KEY TERMS

AutoForm Wizard   An Access tool that creates a form for you without asking you any questions. The form includes all fields in the selected table.

Design view   In this mode, you can design and make changes to the structure of a database.

form   A screen design through which you can look at and modify data stored in a table.

Form view   The mode that Access is in when you view a form on the screen.

index   A field other than the primary key field used to put records in a desired order.

normalizing a database   The process of dividing redundant information into separate databases.

points   Typographical measurement of row height and fonts; one point is equal to 1/72 inch.

primary key   A field in the table that uniquely identifies each record.

record indicator   In Datasheet view, a pencil or other symbol to the left of the record you're working on.

table definition   A listing of the structure of a data table.

Table Wizard   An Access tool that simplifies the process of creating a table structure by asking you questions.

EXERCISES

SHORT ANSWER

1. What are the seven steps for planning a database, as discussed in this session?
2. What field types can be defined in a Microsoft Access table structure?
3. Describe two ways you can customize an Access datasheet.
4. What is the difference between Form view, Design view, and Datasheet view?
5. When would you want to insert a row in a table structure?
6. What does it mean to "normalize a database"?
7. What is the procedure for printing a datasheet?
8. What is a primary key?
9. What does the AutoForm Wizard do?
10. How does Access decide the column order in a datasheet?

HANDS-ON

(*Note*: Before working through the following exercises, make sure you have completed the tasks presented in this session. Also, make sure the Advantage Diskette is in drive A: or drive B:.)

1. This exercise practices creating a table structure and entering a few records.
   a. Open SPORTING.MDB from the Advantage Diskette that is stored in either drive A: or drive B:. (*Note*: You created SPORTING.MDB in this session.)
   b. Create a new table using the table structure listed below:

Field Name	Data Type	Description
Sales Representative ID	Text	Unique four-letter identification code based on the sales rep's name
Last Name	Text	
First Name	Text	
Middle Initial	Text	
Date Hired	Date/Time	
Vacation Days	Number	
Base Salary	Number	

   c. Define the Last Name field as the primary key field.

    d. Choose <u>F</u>ile, Save <u>A</u>s to save the table structure as Sales Representatives.

    e. Click the Datasheet button (or choose <u>V</u>iew, Data<u>s</u>heet) and then add the followin records:

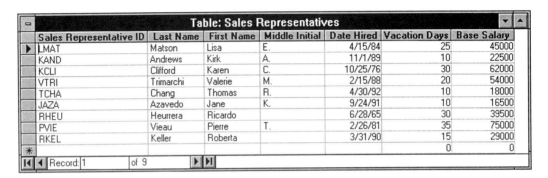

Sales Representative ID	Last Name	First Name	Middle Initial	Date Hired	Vacation Days	Base Salary
LMAT	Matson	Lisa	E.	4/15/84	25	45000
KAND	Andrews	Kirk	A.	11/1/89	10	22500
KCLI	Clifford	Karen	C.	10/25/76	30	62000
VTRI	Trimarchi	Valerie	M.	2/15/88	20	54000
TCHA	Chang	Thomas	R.	4/30/92	10	18000
JAZA	Azavedo	Jane	K.	9/24/91	10	16500
RHEU	Heurrera	Ricardo		6/28/65	30	39500
PVIE	Vieau	Pierre	T.	2/26/81	35	75000
RKEL	Keller	Roberta		3/31/90	15	29000
					0	0

Record: 1   of 9

    f. Change the column widths of each column in the Sales Representatives table so that the <u>B</u>est Fit option is in effect.

    g. Close the Sales Representatives window so that the initial Database window displays. (*Note:* Choose <u>Y</u>es when prompted to save the layout.)

2. This exercise practices creating a table structure and entering a few records.

    a. Open WEDDING.MDB from the Advantage Diskette that is stored in either drive A: or drive B:.

    b. Create a new table using the table structure appearing in Figure 2.10.

Figure 2.10

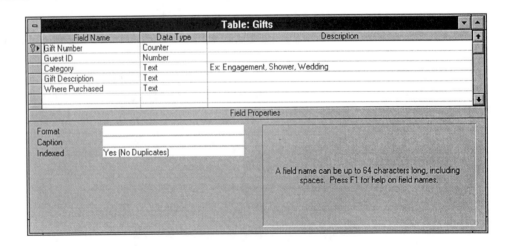

Table: Gifts

Field Name	Data Type	Description
Gift Number	Counter	
Guest ID	Number	
Category	Text	Ex: Engagement, Shower, Wedding
Gift Description	Text	
Where Purchased	Text	

Field Properties

Format
Caption
Indexed   Yes (No Duplicates)

A field name can be up to 64 characters long, including spaces. Press F1 for help on field names.

    c. Define the Gift Number field as the primary key field.

    d. Choose <u>F</u>ile, Save <u>A</u>s to save the table structure as Gifts.

e. Click the Datasheet button (or choose <u>V</u>iew, Data<u>s</u>heet) and then add the following five records:

Gift Number	Guest ID	Category	Gift Description	Where Purchased
1	21	Kitchen Shower	Set of knives	Latham's
2	19	Kitchen Shower	Baking Utensils	The Napa Kitchen
3	5	Engagement	Teacup - blue floral	Giordi's
4	3	Kitchen Shower	Set of mixing bowls	The Napa Kitchen
5	87	Engagement	Book - "Getaways"	Brian's Bookstore
(Counter)	0			

Record: 3   of 5

(*Note*: The Gift Number will be entered automatically. Just press Tab to bypass that field.)

f. Change the displayed font to 10 point and then widen columns to fit, as necessary.
g. Change the row height for all the columns so that it is larger.
h. Close the Gifts window so that the initial Database window displays. Choose <u>N</u>o when prompted to save the layout changes.
i. "Giordi's" has changed its name to "Monde Boutique." Display the Gifts datasheet and edit the third record by changing "Giordi's" to "Monde Boutique."
j. Close the Gifts window.

3. In the last exercise, you created a table in the WEDDING.MDB database called Gifts. Perform the following steps using the Gifts table:

a. Use the AutoForm Wizard to create a form for the Gifts table. When finished, the form should look like Figure 2.11.

Figure 2.11

The Gifts form. This form was created with the AutoForm Wizard and is used with the Gifts table.

Gifts	
Gift Number:	1
Guest ID:	21
Category:	Kitchen Shower
Gift Description:	Set of knives
Where Purchased:	Latham's

Record: 1   of 5

b. Save the form as "Gift Entry Form."
c. Move the record pointer to the bottom of the Gifts table and then enter records 6–9, as shown below:

Gift Number:	Guest ID:	Category:	Gift Description:	Where Purchased:
1	21	Kitchen Shower	Set of knives	Latham's
2	19	Kitchen Shower	Baking Utensils	The Napa Kitchen
3	5	Engagement	Teacup - blue floral	Monde Boutique
4	3	Kitchen Shower	Set of mixing bowls	The Napa Kitchen
5	87	Engagement	Book - "Getaways"	Brian's Bookstore
6	15	Wedding	China Place Setting	Monde Boutique
7	2	Engagement	Teacup - blue rim	Monde Boutique
8	14	Wedding	Wooden Ice Bucket	The Napa Kitchen
9	19	Engagement	Teacup - Green rim	The Napa Kitchen
(Counter)	0			

Record: 6   of 9

d. Close the Form window so that the initial Database window is displaying.

4. In this exercise, you practice customizing the layout of the Gifts datasheet that is stored in the WEDDING.MDB database file. (*Note*: You created the Gifts table in exercise 1 and added data to it in exercises 1 and 2.)
a. Open the WEDDING.MDB database and then display the Gifts datasheet.
b. Widen the Gift Description and Where Purchased columns to accommodate the data.
c. Move the Guest ID column so that it displays before the Gift Number column.
d. Print the Gifts datasheet.
e. Choose File, Save Table to save the new datasheet layout.
f. Close the Gifts window and the WEDDING.MDB database.

SESSION 3

MICROSOFT ACCESS 2.0 FOR WINDOWS: RETRIEVING INFORMATION

One of the primary advantages of a computerized database is the ability to retrieve and display specific information quickly and easily. Rather than searching through endless filing cabinets to compile a list of all your customers in San Francisco, you simply enter a criteria statement and let Microsoft Access do the work for you. In this session, you retrieve, organize, and summarize information from a database.

PREVIEW

When you have completed this session, you will be able to:

Find specific records in a table.

•

Create, save, and print a query.

•

Specify search criteria.

•

Sort dynaset records.

•

Relate multiple tables in a query.

SESSION OUTLINE

Why Is This Session Important?
Finding Records
Query Fundamentals
      Opening a New Query
      The Query Window
      Adding Fields and Widening Columns
      Inserting and Deleting Fields
      Specifying Search Criteria
      Saving the Query Form
      Using Conditional Search Criteria
      Sorting Dynaset Records
      Modifying a Query
      Performing Calculations
      Printing a Dynaset
Querying Multiple Tables
Summary
      Command Summary
Key Terms
Exercises
      Short Answer
      Hands-On

WHY IS THIS SESSION IMPORTANT?

Microsoft Access provides a variety of commands for viewing data. In earlier sessions, you chose View, Datasheet from the Menu bar or clicked the Datasheet button to view all the records in a table. In this session, you learn how to find particular records in a data table and move the record pointer to them, and to create queries to extract and display only specific records and fields. The query procedures illustrated in this session enable you to retrieve information quickly for onscreen and printed reports.

Before proceeding, make sure the following are true:

1. You have loaded Microsoft Access for Windows.
2. Your Advantage Diskette is inserted into drive A: or drive B:. You will save your work onto the diskette and retrieve files that have been created for you. (*Note*: The Advantage Diskette can be duplicated by copying all of the files from your instructor's Master Advantage Diskette.)

FINDING RECORDS

For moving the cursor to a particular record and for performing quick searches when viewing or editing a table, you choose Edit, Find from the Menu bar after displaying a datasheet. Then type in the text you're searching for, using wildcard characters, if necessary. For example, if you're not sure whether to search for Schuler, Inc. or Schuler and Co., search for Schuler*.

Perform the following steps to practice using the FIND command:

1. Open the SPORTING Database window.
    CLICK:
    SELECT: *the drive that contains the Advantage Diskette in the Drives text box*
    SELECT: SPORTING.MDB
    PRESS: Enter or CLICK: OK
    The Database window is displaying.

2. To display the contents of the Customer table:
    DOUBLE-CLICK: Customer table name
    The Customer datasheet should be displaying.

3. To position the cursor in the Company Name field:
    PRESS: [Tab]

4. To search for Schuler*:
    CHOOSE: Edit, Find
    The following dialog box should be displaying:

    Note: Unless you click All Fields button, Access only searches in the
    current column.

5. TYPE: Schuler* *in the Find What text box*
    CLICK: Find Next button
    The cursor should be highlighting "Schuler and Co." in the Company
    Name field. (*Note*: The Find dialog box may be covering the currently
    selected field. If necessary, click on the Title bar and drag it to another
    location.)

6. Even though there aren't any additional occurrences of "Schuler and
    Co.":
    CLICK: Find Next button
    The following dialog box should now be displaying:

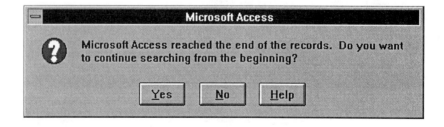

    In response to the prompt:
    CLICK: No
    CLICK: OK

CLICK: Close *to display the datasheet*
Notice that the record pointer has moved to the "Schuler and Co." record.

7. To display the Database window:
   CHOOSE: File, Close

Especially with large databases, the FIND command can save you time when you need to move the record pointer to a particular record so you can edit it.

Quick Reference *Finding Records*	1. Display the datasheet.
	2. Position the cursor in the column you want to search.
	3. CHOOSE: Edit, Find
	4. TYPE: the text you're searching for into the Find What text box CLICK: Find Next button
	5. When you're finished with a search: CLICK: No CLICK: OK CLICK: Close *to display the datasheet*

QUERY FUNDAMENTALS

A query is a question you ask of your database, such as "How many customers live in Chicago?" or "What products did XYZ Corporation purchase last year?" In this section, you learn how to build queries in the Query window and to display the result of the queries you create. As you learned in Session 1, the result of a query is called a **dynaset**.

With Access, you can create select queries and action queries. A **select query** lets you ask questions of your database and display the dynaset results in a datasheet. You can create four types of **action queries**, which automatically perform an action on the data in a dynaset: (1) **update query**, which updates the data in a dynaset, (2) **append query**, which adds the data in a dynaset to another table, (3) **delete query**, which deletes the records in a dynaset from one or more tables, and (4) **make table query**, which creates a new table from a dynaset. In this session, we focus on select queries.

OPENING A NEW QUERY

To create a query, you must open a database into the Database window and then click the Query button. You then need to tell Access what table(s) you want to include in the query. In this section you will base your queries on one table, the Customer table, which is a part of the SPORTING.MDB file. Later in this session, we lead you through basing a query on two tables.

Perform the following steps:

1. If you completed the last section, the SPORTING Database window should be displaying.

2. To create a query:
   CLICK: Query button *(located on the left side of the Database window)*
   CLICK: New button
   At this point, you have the choice of either creating the query from scratch or using a **Query Wizard** to simplify the process of creating the query. For most common queries you don't need to use the Query Wizard. We'd like to lead you through creating a query from scratch. You will then have the understanding necessary to take advantage of all that the Query Wizard feature has to offer. To learn more about the Query Wizard feature, choose Help, Search from the Menu bar and type wizards.

3. CLICK: New Query
   The Add Table dialog box is displaying. Access is waiting for you to choose a table to use in your queries.

4. SELECT: the Customer table name
   CLICK: Add button
   (*Note*: You could have just double-clicked the Customer table name.)
   CLICK: Close button *to close the Add Table dialog box*
   The Query window should look similar to Figure 3.1. We describe the Query window in the next section.

Figure 3.1
The Query window
after selecting the
Customer table

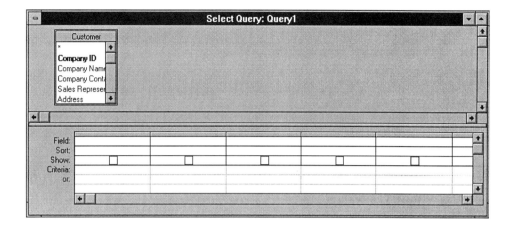

Quick Reference	1. In the Database window:
Create a New	CLICK: Query button
Query	CLICK: New button
	CLICK: New Query
	2. Select one or more tables to base your query on by clicking the Add button.
	3. Proceed by defining the query.

THE QUERY WINDOW

The Query window is a graphical **query-by-example (QBE)** tool, because you in effect draw a picture of your query in the QBE grid by choosing fields and typing in record criteria. Because this window is graphically oriented, you can use the mouse to drag field name objects into the QBE grid.

The top half of the Query window displays the tables that you'll base your query on. The bottom half of the window contains the QBE grid that you use to define your query. Add a field to the QBE grid by dragging its name from the field list on the top of the Query window into the Field row. The rest of the rows on the QBE grid are used to refine your queries, and are described on the next page:

- Sort   Use this option to sort the dynaset into order by the field in this column. By clicking the arrow in the Sort box, you can specify Ascending, Descending, or No Sort. (*Note*: Sorting is used to put a dynaset into order whereas the primary key is used to put the underlying data table into order.) It takes Access less time to sort a dynaset that has been indexed on the sort field.

- Show   By clicking in the Show box, you specify whether to show/not show the field in the dynaset. When the box is empty, the field will display in the dynaset.

- Criteria   Use this option to be selective about the records that display in the dynaset. For example, by setting a criteria, you can list the companies (from the Customer table) located in Minnesota by typing `Minnesota` into the Criteria row. You learn how to use this field shortly.

- or   Use this option to specify another criteria. For example, you can list the companies located in Minnesota (using the Criteria row) *or* Illinois by typing `Illinois` into the Or row. As a result, the dynaset will contain records for companies in either Minnesota or Illinois.

Notice that you can't see all the field names in the Customer table object located on the top half of the Query window. When using Access, you often have to size windows and objects to meet your needs. To resize an object, point to the object's border until the pointer looks like a double-ended arrow. Then click and hold down the mouse, and drag the object border in the desired direction.

Perform the following steps to resize the Customer table object:

1. Point to the right edge of the Customer table object until the pointer changes shape to look like a double-ended arrow.

2. Click and hold down the left mouse button and then drag the mouse to the right until you see the widest field name (Sales Representative ID).

3. Notice that you can only see the first few field names. To see additional field names, drag the thumb down the vertical scroll bar in the Customer table object.

4. Now drag the thumb to the very top of the vertical scroll bar. The Customer table object should look similar to the following:

An asterisk (*) is displaying. When the asterisk is dragged down into the QBE grid, all fields are included in the dynaset. Also notice that Company ID is bolded; this indicates that the Company ID field is the primary key (you defined the primary key in Session 2).

ADDING FIELDS AND WIDENING COLUMNS

In this section, you will add the Company Name, Company Contact, City, and Phone fields to the QBE grid. Perform the following steps:

1. Point to the Company Name field name in the Customer table object and drag the name down into the Field box located in the first column of the QBE grid. When you release the mouse button, "Company Name" should display in the Field box. (*Note*: You could have also clicked the arrow in the Field box and then selected Company Name.)

2. Drag the Company Contact field name into the second column of the QBE grid.

3. Drag the City field name into the third column of the QBE grid.

4. Drag the Phone field name into the fourth column of the QBE grid. The Query window should look like Figure 3.2.

Figure 3.2
Four fields have
been added to the
QBE grid.

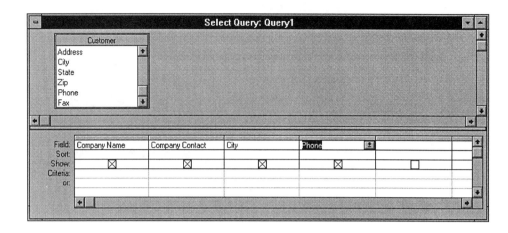

5. To view the datasheet:
    CHOOSE: View, Datasheet, or

    CLICK: Datasheet view button (▦)
    The Company Name, Company Contact, City, and Phone fields should
    be displaying in the datasheet. You'll widen the Company Name and
    Company Contact columns in the next step.

It is important that you know that if you edit the field data in the dynaset,
the underlying data table is changed also. For example, if you change the
name displaying in the Company Contact field of one or more records, the
name will be changed in the underlying data table. If you're aware of this
feature, it can be very useful; otherwise you might accidentally alter data.

6. To widen the Company Name column, point with the mouse to the
    right of the field heading until the mouse pointer looks like a vertical
    bar with a horizontal arrow through it. Drag the column separator to
    the right until you can see the field contents. (*Note*: You may need to
    periodically widen columns in a datasheet.)

7. By double-clicking the column separator, instead of dragging it, you
    can widen the column to the "best fit." Point with the mouse pointer to
    the column separator to the right of the Company Contact field name
    and then double-click. The column should have widened.

8. To view the query in Design view:
    CHOOSE: View, Query Design, or

    CLICK: Design view button (▨)

9. Continue on to the next two sections to learn how to insert and delete
    fields and specify search criteria.

Quick Reference	While displaying the Query window:
Adding Fields to the QBE Grid	• Point to the field name in the appropriate table object and then drag it into the Field box in the QBE grid, or • Click the arrow in the Field box of the QBE grid and then select the appropriate field.

Quick Reference	Position the mouse pointer on the appropriate column separator and
Widening a Column in the Dynaset	then drag it in the desired direction, or double-click to assume the "best fit" width.

INSERTING AND DELETING FIELDS

Once you've added fields to the QBE grid, you may decide that you want to insert a column in the grid so that you can add another field. To accomplish this, drag a field name into the Field row of the QBE grid where you want the field to be inserted. The field will be inserted at the pointer position. To delete a column from the QBE grid, click in the column you want to delete and then choose Edit, Delete Column. (*Note*: If you don't want to delete a column from the QBE grid, but don't want it to display in the dynaset, click Show in the QBE grid.)

Quick Reference	• Drag a field into the QBE grid where you want it to be positioned. The field will be inserted in the QBE grid.
Inserting/Deleting Columns on the QBE Grid	• Click in the column that you want to delete. Then choose Edit, Delete Column.

SPECIFYING SEARCH CRITERIA

Querying a database involves more than limiting its display to specific fields. You usually want to extract records from the table that meet a given condition. Imagine being able to display a customer's purchase history with a few simple keystrokes. And doing this all while talking to them on the phone!

To limit the records that display in a datasheet, you enter a **conditional statement** in the QBE grid in the Criteria row. A conditional statement can be one of several forms. First, you can enter an example of the value that you are looking for. For example, to retrieve all your customers who live in Stockton, you simply type Stockton in the Criteria row of the City column in the QBE grid. Second, you can use mathematical operators to limit records between a given range of values. In other words, in an

Employee database, you could type >01/01/94 into the Hired Date column of the QBE grid to produce a list of all employees hired since January 1, 1994. Lastly, you can use wildcard charcacters to retrieve information. The question mark (?) is used to represent a single character, and the asterisk (*) is used to represent one or more characters. For example, to display those records for companies whose names begin with the letters "st" or "ST", such as "Steiner's" or "Sturgeon Foods", type st* in the Company Name field. (*Note*: Typing St* is the same as typing st*.) The more common mathematical query operators and wildcard character examples are summarized in Table 3.1.

Table 3.1	*COMMAND*	*TASK*
Access Query Operators	>	Greater than; finds values that are greater than the specified value. For example, >5000 finds all records where the field value is greater than 5,000. (*Note*: You do not enter commas in numeric queries.)
	<	Less than; finds values less than the specified value. For example, <12/31/92 retrieves all records where the field value is less than December 31, 1992.
	>=	Greater than or equal to; finds values greater than or equal to the specified value. For example, >=Moser retrieves all records where the field value starts with "Moser" and then continues to the end of the alphabet.
	<=	Less than or equal to; finds values less than or equal to the specified value. For example, <=98000 retrieves all records where the field value (perhaps a ZIP code) contains 98000 or lower.
	Between *Value1* And *Value2*	List those records that contain values between *Value1* and *Value2*.
	Value1 Or *Value2*	List those records that have either *Value1* or *Value2*.
	Not *Value1*	List those records that don't have *Value1*.

Wildcard Character Examples	Like Sm?th	List those records in which the field begins with "Sm", has a single character in the middle of the name, and ends with "th". Example: Smyth, Smith
	Like Ch*ng	List those records in which the field begins with "Ch", has one or more characters in the middle of the name, and ends with "ng". Example: Chang, Chickering
	Like *on*	List those records in which the field has "on" in the middle of the field. Example: Conditional, Conference, Monday
	Like */*/93	List those records which end with 93 in the date field

Access gives you quite a bit of flexibility when entering expressions into the Criteria field. For example, to list those customers in Stockton, you could type:

- `Stockton`
- `=Stockton`
- `"Stockton"`
- `="Stockton"`

In the above example, Access would display "Stockton" with the quotes in the QBE grid. If the text you're searching for contains two words, such as San Francisco, you *must* surround the text with quotation marks. After you've typed in search criteria, Access converts it to a standard format. Likewise, if you type "st*" as the search criteria, Access displays the following in the QBE grid: Like "st*"

Perform the following steps to practice specifying search criteria:

1. At this point, we assume that you completed the last section, and that the Query window is displaying with the QBE grid (see Figure 3.2).

2. In this step you will type `San Francisco` in as the criteria for the City field.
   CLICK: the Criteria field in the City column
   TYPE: `"San Francisco"`
   PRESS: (Enter)
   The Query window should look like Figure 3.3.

Figure 3.3

A search criteria
has been typed into
the City column in
the QBE grid.

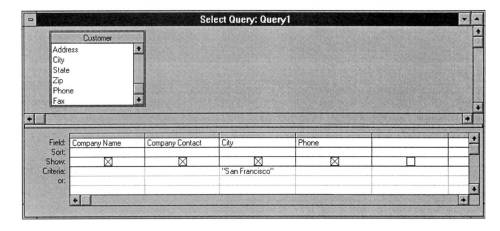

3. To display the datasheet, click the Datasheet button (▦). One record
   should be displaying that meets the criteria.

4. To view the query in Design view:
   CHOOSE: View, Query Design, or

   CLICK: Design view button (▨)
   The Query window should be displaying.

5. In this step, you will type "s*" into the City column in the QBE grid.
   CLICK: the Criteria field in the City column
   PRESS: (Home) *to move the cursor to the left of the field*
   PRESS: (Delete) *until the text in the Criteria field is deleted*
   TYPE: S*
   (*Note*: You don't need quotation marks because you're not typing in
   two words.)
   PRESS: (Enter)
   The Query window should look like Figure 3.4.

Figure 3.4

A new search criteria has been typed into the City column in the QBE grid.

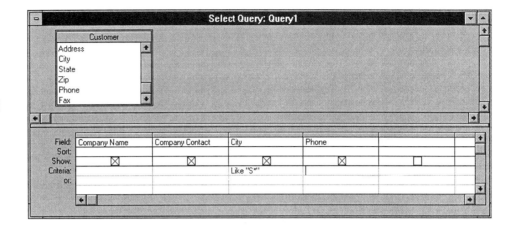

6. To display the datasheet, click the Datasheet button (▦). The screen should look like Figure 3.5.

Figure 3.5

These records meet the criteria displaying in Figure 3.4.

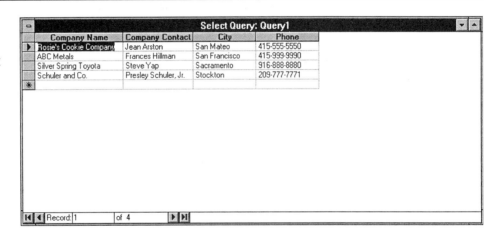

7. To view the query in Design view:
   CHOOSE: View, Query Design, or
   CLICK: Design view button (▨)
   The Query window should be displaying.

8. To delete the criteria in the City field:
   CLICK: the Criteria field in the City column
   PRESS: (Home) *to move the cursor to the left of the field*
   PRESS: (Delete) *until the text in the Criteria field is deleted*
   (*Note*: To delete all the criteria displaying in the Criteria row, you can choose Edit, Delete Row after clicking in the Criteria row. You'll use this procedure shortly.)

9. On your own, perform the following steps:
   a. Type VTRI into the Sales Representative column (in the Criteria field).
   b. Display the datasheet. Two records should be displaying.
   c. Display the Query window in Design view.
   d. Delete the criteria displaying in the Criteria field in the City column.

10. Continue on to the next section so you can save the query form.

Quick Reference	In the Query window, position the cursor in the Criteria row of the QBE
Entering Search Criteria	grid, in the appropriate field column, and type in a conditional statement.

SAVING THE QUERY FORM

In this section you will delete the criteria you entered into the QBE grid in the last section and then save the Query form.

1. The Query window should be displaying.

2. To save the query form:
   CHOOSE: File, Save As *from the Menu bar*
   TYPE: Customer Listing
   PRESS: [Enter]
   (*Note*: A query can't have the same name as the table. You will use this query file in the Modifying a Query section later in this session.)

Quick Reference	In the Query window:
Saving a Query	CHOOSE: File, Save As *from the Menu bar*
	Make sure to give the query a name that is different from the table name.

3. Close the Query window. The Database window should be displaying.

USING CONDITIONAL SEARCH CRITERIA

Using Microsoft Access, you can perform simple and complex query operations. A simple query usually involves extracting information based on a single criteria or condition; you created a simple query in a previous section when you typed "San Francisco" into the City field of the Criteria field. A complex query, on the other hand, involves more than one criteria and employs conditional logic. **Conditional logic** is the method by which criteria statements are joined and executed in a query statement. For example, you may want to produce a list of all your customers from Sacramento who deal with the sales representative with the PVIE identification code (Figure 3.6). This query requires that you join the two criteria using the *logical and* and that the two criteria are entered on the same line.

Figure 3.6

The two criteria entered in the QBE grid represent a *logical and* query.

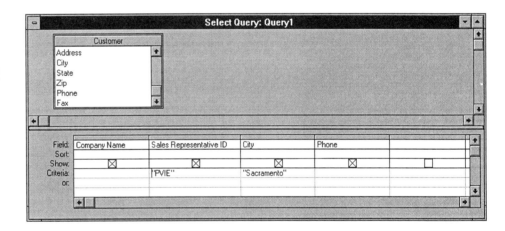

As another example, you may want to find all your customers who live in either Sacramento or Phoenix. Obviously, this query requires a *logical or* statement. For a *logical or* relationship, you can use the Criteria line or the Or line of the QBE grid. For example, in the City column of the QBE grid, you can enter Sacramento or Phoenix on the Criteria line, or you can enter Sacramento on the Criteria line and Phoenix on the Or line. Figures 3.7 and 3.8 show the QBE grid for these two queries; for each query, the resulting datasheet is the same.

Figure 3.7

This *logical or* query
is represented on
the same line.

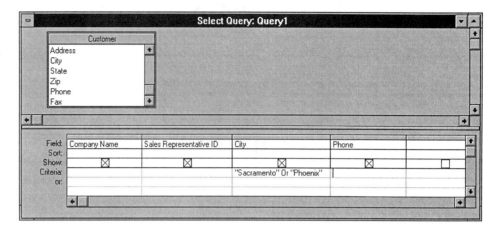

Figure 3.8

This *logical or* query
is represented on
separate lines.

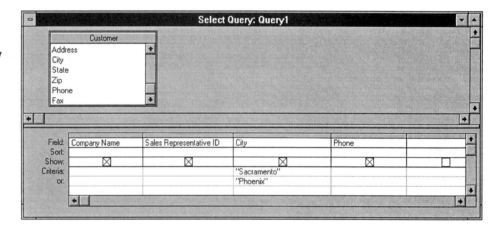

To specify a range of values, use one of two methods. To retrieve all the
records where a sales representative's salary is greater than 40000 and less
than 60000, type >40000 and <60000 on the Criteria line in the Base
Salary column (Figure 3.9). To retrieve those records where a sales
representative's salary is greater than or equal to 40000 and less or equal to
60000, type between 40000 and 60000 on the Criteria line in the
Base Salary column.

Figure 3.9

This *logical and* query represents a range of values.

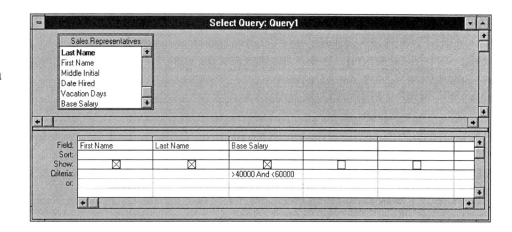

In this section, you will create a query for use with the Sales Representatives table, stored in the SPORTING.MDB database. (*Note*: You created the Sales Representatives table in Hands-On exercise 1 at the end of Session 2.)

1. At this point, we assume that you completed the last section, and that the Database window for the SPORTING.MDB database is displaying.

2. To create a new query:
   CLICK: Query button (*located on the left side of the Database window*)
   CLICK: New button
   CLICK: New Query

3. SELECT: the Sales Representatives table name
   CLICK: Add button
   CLICK: Close button *to close the Add Table dialog box*
   The Query window should be displaying.
   (*Note*: If you want to, drag the sides of the table object so you can see all the field names.)

4. Add the following fields to the QBE grid: Last Name, First Name, Date Hired, Vacation Days, Base Salary. (*Note*: If necessary, to display the last column in the QBE grid so that you can add the Base Salary field, click in the column and then press ⟶.)

In the following steps you will list the sales representatives who have between 10 and 30 vacation days.

1. Click in the Criteria field of the Vacation Days column in the QBE grid.

2. TYPE: between 10 and 30

3. To display the datasheet:
    CHOOSE: View, Datasheet
    or
    CLICK: Datasheet button (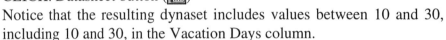)
    Notice that the resulting dynaset includes values between 10 and 30, including 10 and 30, in the Vacation Days column.

4. To view the query in Design view:
    CHOOSE: View, Query Design, or
    CLICK: Design view button (▨)
    The Query window should be displaying.

5. To delete the current criteria:
    CLICK: in the Criteria row
    CHOOSE: Edit, Delete Row

6. To save the query:
    CHOOSE: File, Save
    TYPE: Sales Rep Listing
    PRESS: Enter or CLICK: OK

On your own, enter criteria into the QBE grid so that the records for the following sales representatives display in the datasheet:

*   Sales representatives who have a base salary that is less than 20000

*   Sales representatives who have a base salary that is between 30000 and 50000

*   Sales representatives who have a base salary that is greater than 30000 and less than 50000

7. Close the Query window without saving. The Database window should be displaying.

SORTING DYNASET RECORDS

In this section you create a new query and specify a sort order in the QBE grid. Unless you specify a sort order, dynasets display in the same order that governs the data table, which may or may not be determined by a primary key field.

Perform the following steps:

1. At this point, we assume that you completed the last section, and that the Database window for the SPORTING database is displaying.

2. To create a new query:
    CLICK: Query button (*located on the left side of the Database window*)
    CLICK: New button
    CLICK: New Query

3. SELECT: the Customer table name
    CLICK: Add button
    CLICK: Close button *to close the Add Table dialog box*
    The Query window should be displaying.
    (*Note*: If you want to, drag the sides of the table object so you can see all the field names.)

4. Add the Company ID, Company Contact, and Sales Representative ID fields to the QBE grid.

5. Display the dynaset:
    CHOOSE: View, Datasheet
    or
    CLICK: Datasheet button (▦)
    Since the data table displays in order by the primary key, the Company ID field, the dynaset is now displaying in the order of the Company ID field.

6. To view the query in Design view:
    CHOOSE: View, Query Design, or
    CLICK: Design view button (▧)
    The Query window should be displaying.

7. To display the dynaset in order by the Sales Representative ID field:
    CLICK: the Sort field *in the Sales Representative ID column*
    CLICK: ⊡
    CLICK: Ascending

8. Display the dynaset. The records should now be displaying in order by the Sales Representative ID field.

9. Display the Query window.

Wouldn't it be nice to define a secondary sort key so that the records for each sales representative display in order by the Company ID field? To do this, you must move the Sales Representative ID column so that it displays before the Company ID column. Then specify an ascending sort for the Sales Representative ID field and an ascending sort for the Company ID field.

Perform the following steps:

1. The Query window should be displaying. To select the Sales Representative ID column so you can move it:
    POINT: to just above field name until a downward-pointing arrow displays, and then
    CLICK: with the mouse
    The Sales Representative ID column should be displaying in reverse video.

2. To move the column, point to just above the field name and then click and hold down the mouse button.

3. Drag the field name to the leftmost column of the QBE grid and then release the mouse button.

4. CLICK: the Sort field *in the Company ID column*
    CLICK: ⊡
    CLICK: Ascending

5. Display the dynaset. Notice that the dynaset is in order by the Sales Representative ID column; for each Sales Representative ID, the dynaset is in order by the Company ID field.

6. Choose File, Close to display the Database window and select No when prompted to save the query.

Quick Reference	In the Query window, position the cursor in the Sort row of the QBE grid,
Sorting a Dynaset	in the appropriate field column, and click. Then click the arrow and
	select Ascending, Descending, or "(not sorted)".

MODIFYING A QUERY

In this section you will modify a query named Customer Listing that you created earlier in this session. You will modify the query so that it is sorted into order by the City field.

1. At this point, we assume that you completed the last section, and that the Database window for the SPORTING database is displaying.

2. To modify the Customer Listing query:
    CLICK: the Query button
    DOUBLE-CLICK: Customer Listing query name
    The Customer Listing dynaset should be listing.

3. To display the dynaset in sorted order:
    CHOOSE: View, Query Design, or

    CLICK: Design view button (📝)
    The Query window should be displaying.

4. CLICK: the Sort field *in the City column*
    CLICK: [±]
    CLICK: Ascending

5. Display the dynaset:
    CHOOSE: View, Datasheet
    or

    CLICK: Datasheet button (▦)
    The dynaset should be displaying in order by the City field.

6. Now that you've modified the query, save it by choosing File, Save Query.

7. Close the current window so that the SPORTING Database window is displaying.

Quick Reference *Modify a Query*	1. In the Database window, click the Query button and double-click the name of the query that you want to modify.
	2. Display the query in Design view and make changes to the QBE grid.
	3. CHOOSE: File, Save Query

PERFORMING CALCULATIONS

Besides performing searches on table data, you can perform calculations on textual and numeric data to find summary information on all the records in a table or selected records. For example, you might want to determine the average number of vacation days given to each sales representative. Before performing a calculation, you must display the Total row in the QBE grid by choosing View, Totals from the Menu bar. Table 3.2 describes the different types of calculations that you can perform in Access. (*Note*: To learn more about performing calculations, choose Help, Search and then type totals.)

Table 3.2

Access Calculations

CALCULATION	DESCRIPTION
Sum	Display the total of values stored in a field.
Avg	Display the average of values stored in a field.
Min	Display the lowest value stored in a field.
Max	Display the highest value stored in a field.
Count	The number of entries in a field (not including null values)
StDev	Display the standard deviation of values stored in a field.
Var	Display the variance of values stored in a field.
First	The field value of the first record in the table or query.
Last	The field value of the last record in the table or query.

Perform the following steps to perform a calculation on all the records in a table:

1. If you completed the last section, the SPORTING Database window is displaying.
    CLICK: Query button
    CLICK: New
    CLICK: New Query

2. SELECT: Sales Representatives table name
    CLICK: Add
    CLICK: Close

3. Drag the Vacation Days and Base Salary field names into the QBE grid.

4. To display the Total row in the QBE grid:
    CHOOSE: View, Totals
    The QBE grid should look like the following:

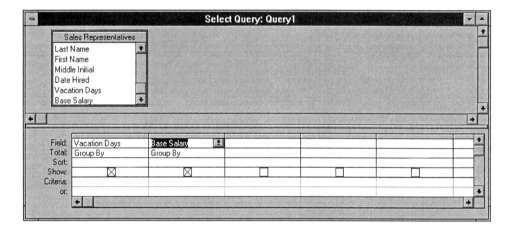

5. Since you're performing a calculation on *all* the records in the table, you don't want "Group By" to be displaying in the total row. To determine the average number of vacation days, for *each* field you must select Avg in the Totals row:
    CLICK: Total field *of the Vacation Days field*
    CLICK: [⬇]
    SELECT: Avg
    CLICK: Total field *of the Base Salary field*
    CLICK: [⬇]
    SELECT: Avg

6. To display the result of the calculations:
    CLICK: 🔳
    When you perform a calculation, Access displays the results in the form of a "snapshot," a type of dynaset that you can't update (see below).

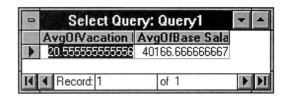

    Notice that the numbers are displaying with many trailing decimal places; you will correct this shortly.

7. To display the query in Design view:
    CLICK: 📐

8. To display the field properties so you can control the display of trailing decimal places:
    CLICK: *in the Vacation Days column of the QBE grid*
    CHOOSE: Yiew, Properties
    CLICK: Format
    CLICK: ▼
    SELECT: Fixed
    CLICK: Decimal Places field
    CLICK: ▼
    SELECT: 0

9. With the Field Properties box displaying:
    CLICK: *in the Base Salary column of the QBE grid*
    CLICK: Format
    CLICK: ▼
    SELECT: Fixed
    CLICK: Decimal Places field
    CLICK: ▼
    SELECT: 0

10. To display the results of the calculations:
    CLICK: 🔳
    The dynaset should look like the following:

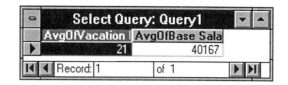

In the following steps, you will perform calculations on selected records in a table; to accomplish this, you must use the "Group By" expression in the Total row of the QBE grid. You will determine the average base salary of those individuals who receive 10 vacation days per year.

1. If you completed the last section, the dynaset should be displaying. To display the query in Design view:
    CLICK: ▨

2. To remove the Field Properties box:
    CHOOSE: <u>V</u>iew, <u>P</u>roperties

3. Since you want to base your search on the Vacation Days column, "Group By" must be displaying in the total row.
    CLICK: Totals field *of the Vacation Days field*
    CLICK: ⬇
    DRAG: the scroll bar upwards
    SELECT: Group By

4. To determine the average Base Salary of those individuals who receive 10 vacation days per year:
    CLICK: Criteria row *of the Vacation Days field*
    TYPE: 10
    The Query window should look like the following:

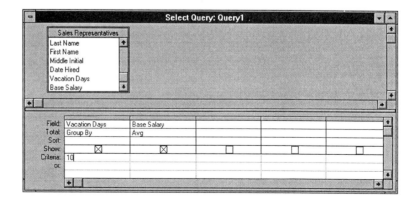

5. To display the result of the calculations:
   CLICK: ▦
   The answer "19000" should be displaying. That is, $19,000 is the average salary for individuals receiving 10 vacation days per year.

6. Close the current window without saving. The SPORTING Database window should be displaying. To learn more about printing, continue on to the next section.

Quick Reference
 Perform
 Calculations in a
 Query
	1. In Design view:
	    CHOOSE: View, Totals
	 2. Click in the Total row, click ⬆, and then select a calculation to
	    perform.

PRINTING A DYNASET

To print a dynaset or table, first display the dynaset or table and then choose File, Print to display the Print dialog box. Then press [Enter] or click OK to print all the records in the entire dynaset or table.

If the records are too wide to fit across the width of the page, you may want to select Setup from the Print dialog box and then click the Landscape button. Then press [Enter] or click OK to display the Print dialog box again. If the records are still too wide to fit on the page, Access prints the first group of fields on the first page and the remaining fields on the next page.

To print a selection of adjacent records from a dynaset, first select the records by positioning the mouse pointer to the left of the first field in the dynaset until it looks like a right-pointing arrow; that is, the pointer shouldn't look like a bar with a vertical arrow through it. Then drag the mouse down to select the records. Then click the Selection button from the Print dialog box before printing.

Perform the following steps to print the results of a query:

1. The SPORTING Database window should be displaying.
   CLICK: the Query button
   DOUBLE-CLICK: Customer Listing query name
   The Customer Listing dynaset should be displaying.

2. To print the dynaset:
   CHOOSE: File, Print
   PRESS: (Enter) or CLICK: OK

3. Choose File, Close to display the Database window.

QUERYING MULTIPLE TABLES

In this section you will add two tables (the Customer and Sales Representatives tables) to the Query window, define a relationship between them, and then add selected fields from each table to the QBE grid. Both data tables must have a field in common before you can establish a relationship between the tables. To Access's credit, this sophisticated procedure is very easy to perform.

Perform the following steps to define a relationship between the Customer and Sales Representatives tables so that for each company you can see the full name of Sporting, Inc.'s sales representative, rather than just the Sales Representative ID code. The relationship between these two fields is based on the Sales Representative ID field.

1. At this point, we assume that you completed the last section, and that the Database window for the SPORTING database is displaying.

2. To create a new query:
   CLICK: Query button (*located on the left side of the Database window*)
   CLICK: New button
   CLICK: New Query

3. SELECT: the Customer table name
   CLICK: Add button
   SELECT: the Sales Representatives table name
   CLICK: Add button
   CLICK: Close button *to close the Add Table dialog box*
   The Query window should be displaying.
   (*Note*: If you want to, drag the sides of the table objects so you can see all the field names.)

At this point you must define a relationship between the two tables. This relationship will be based on the Sales Representative ID field since both tables have this field in common.

4. Point to the Sales Representative ID field in the Customer table and then drag it over to the Sales Representative ID field in the Sales Representatives table. A line should now connect the two Sales Representative ID fields (Figure 3.10). (*Note*: In Figure 3.10, the table objects have been resized to more easily see the joining line.)

Figure 3.10

The Customer and Sales Representatives tables are joined on the Sales Representative ID field.

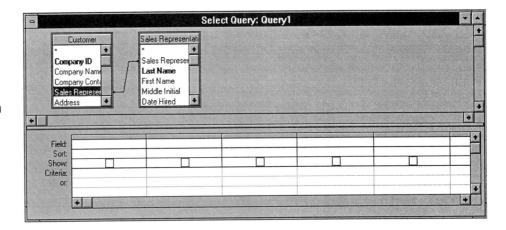

5. Add the Company Name and Company Contact fields from the Customer table to the QBE grid.

6. Add the First Name and Last Name fields from the Sales Representatives table to the QBE grid.

7. Display the dynaset:
    CHOOSE: View, Datasheet
    or
    CLICK: Datasheet button (▦)
    Note that for each company you can see the full name of the sales representative. The dynaset is currently grouped by the Sales Representative ID field (even though that field isn't included in the dynaset).

8. To view the query in Design view:
    CLICK: ▧
    The Query window should be displaying.

9. So that you know what table each field in the QBE grid comes from:
   CHOOSE: View, Table Names

10. To display the dynaset in order by the Company Name field:
    CLICK: the Sort field *in the Company Name column of the QBE grid*
    CLICK: [±]
    CLICK: Ascending
    The Query window should look like Figure 3.11.

Figure 3.11

The Query window.

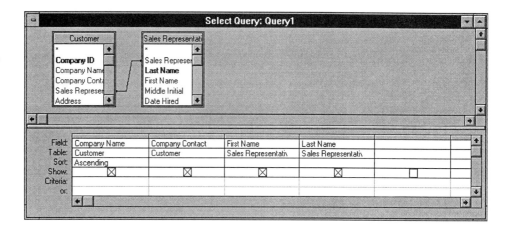

11. Display the datasheet:
    CLICK: [▦]
    The datasheet should be displaying in order by the Company Name field.

12. Choose File, Close to display the Database window and select No when prompted to save the query.

Quick Reference *Querying Multiple Tables*	1. In the Database window: CLICK: Query button CLICK: New button 2. CLICK: New Query 3. Select one or more tables to base your query on by clicking the Add button. Click Close when finished. 4. Drag the joining field name from the first table object to the same joining field name in the next table object. 5. Add fields from each table to the QBE grid and sort the dynaset (optional).

SUMMARY

In this session, you learned how to find table records and to create, customize, and modify queries. Specifically, you learned how to use the QBE grid in the Query window to be specific about the fields and records that display in the datasheet. You also learned how to perform calculations in a query and include more than one table in a query.

COMMAND SUMMARY

Table 3.3 provides a list of the commands and procedures covered in this session.

	COMMAND	TASK
Table 3.3 Command Summary	Edit, Find	Find records in a datasheet
	In the Database window, click Query button, New, New Query	Create a new query
	File, Save As	Save a query form
	In the QBE grid, click Sort field, select a sorting option	Sort a dynaset
	In Design view, View, Totals	Include the Total row in the QBE grid so you can perform calculations
	View, Properties	View the Field Properties dialog box
	File, Print	Print a table or dynaset
	View, Table Names	Display the originating table name in the QBE grid

KEY TERMS

action query   With this query type, you ask questions of a database and, depending on the results, Access performs an action that changes one or more objects in the database.

append query   A type of action query that adds data to a table.

conditional logic   The method by which criteria statements are joined and executed in a query statement.

conditional statement   A query statement that limits the number of records that display in the datasheet.

delete query   A type of action query that deletes records in a dynaset from one or more tables.

dynaset   In Access, the result of a query.

make table query   A type of action query that creates a new table from a dynaset.

query-by-example (QBE)   Querying by drawing a picture of a query in the QBE grid by choosing fields and typing in record criteria.

Query Wizard   An Access tool that can simplify the process of creating a query.

select query   With this query type, you ask questions of your database and display the dynaset results in a datasheet.

update query   A type of action query that updates data in a table.

EXERCISES

SHORT ANSWER

1. When would you want to choose Edit, Find from the Menu bar?
2. What is a dynaset?
3. What is the difference between a select query and an action query?
4. From the Database window, how do you create a new query?
5. What kinds of calculations can you perform in an Access query?
6. What is the purpose of the Criteria row in the QBE grid?

7. While displaying the Query window that includes a field named Company in the QBE grid, how would you sort the dynaset into ascending order by the Company field?

8. If you are displaying a query in Design view, how do you then display the dynaset?

9. To relate two tables together in the Query window, what must you do?

10. What is the purpose of the QBE grid?

HANDS-ON

(*Note*: In the following exercises, save your work onto and open files from the Advantage Diskette.)

1. Open the TRAINING database that is stored on the Advantage Diskette. Perform the following steps:
   a. Create a new query for use with the Students table.
   b. Include the following fields in the query: First Name, Last Name, Company, City, and Phone.
   c. Display the datasheet.
   d. Display the Query window.
   e. Type in a criteria so that only students who live in San Diego will list in the dynaset. Display the datasheet.
   f. Close the Query window without saving.

2. Open the TRAINING database. Do the following to modify a query:
   a. CLICK: Query button
      SELECT: Student Listing name
      CLICK: Open button
   b. Display the Student Listing query in Design view.
   c. Move the Last Name field so that it displays before the First Name field.
   d. Sort the query into ascending order so that the datasheet is in order by the Last Name field, and for all last names, the datasheet is in order by the First Name field.
   e. Display the datasheet.
   f. Save the modified query.

3. Open the TRAINING database. Do the following to create a multiple-table query:
   a. Create a query that includes the Courses and Instructors tables.
   b. Link the two tables on the Instructor ID field.
   c. Include the Title and Location fields from the Courses table, and the First Name and Last Name fields from the Instructors table.

    d. Display table names in the QBE grid.

    e. Display the datasheet.

    f. Save the query as "Instructor Summary Sheet."

4. Open the WEDDING database. Do the following to create a multiple-table query:

    a. Create a query that includes the Guest List and Gifts tables. (*Note*: You created the Gifts table in Session 2 Hands-On exercise 2.)

    b. Link the two tables on the Guest ID field.

    c. Include the First Name and Last Name fields from the Guest List table, and the Gift Description and Where Purchased fields from the Gifts table.

    d. Display table names in the QBE grid.

    e. Display the datasheet. Notice that the datasheet isn't displaying in any particular order.

    f. Display the Query window and then sort the datasheet into order by the Last Name field.

    g. Display the datasheet and then save the query as "Gifts Received."

MICROSOFT ACCESS 2.0 FOR WINDOWS: PRESENTING YOUR DATA

The purpose of a database management system is to turn data into information. Using the thousands of invoices that may be entered into a data table each month, for example, the income statement and accounts receivable report summarize and present that data as information. Each day, people make business decisions using reports obtained from database management systems. This session shows you how to create and edit reports for presenting your Access data.

PREVIEW

When you have completed this session, you will be able to:

Use the Report Wizard to create reports.

•

Create mailing labels.

•

Preview and print reports.

•

Design a report by:

Editing control text.
Resizing controls.
Moving controls.
Adding a graphic to a report.

SESSION OUTLINE

Why Is This Session Important?
Creating Reports with the Report Wizard
      AutoReport
      Groups/Totals Report
      Mailing Labels Report
Designing a Report
      Understanding Reports
      Editing Control Text
      Resizing Controls
      Moving Controls
      Adding a Graphic to a Report
Summary
      Command Summary
Key Terms
Exercises
      Short Answer
      Hands-On

WHY IS THIS SESSION IMPORTANT?

In Session 2, you learned how to view table data using a form. Forms are useful for viewing at once all the fields in a record so you can edit or add table data; you learn more about creating and editing forms in Session 5. In Session 3, you learned how to view table data using a query. You learned that queries are useful for viewing selected fields, and records that meet your criteria. For example, using a query, you can list those records that pertain to a particular sales representative; you turn raw data into meaningful information.

In this session, you learn how to create **reports** in order to "dress up" your table data or query results so they can be included in a formal presentation. In a report, you can use such design elements as text, data, graphics (such as a chart or picture), lines, and borders. You decide what design elements to include. Examples of reports are sales summaries, invoices, mailing labels, and inventory listings.

Fortunately, Access provides you with the **Report Wizard** tool, described in the next section, to simplify the process of designing a report. Even experienced users often create a report using the Report Wizard and then customize the report using commands and procedures described later in this learning guide.

Before proceeding, make sure the following are true:

1. You have loaded Microsoft Access for Windows.
2. Your Advantage Diskette is inserted into drive A: or drive B:. You will save your work onto the diskette and retrieve files that have been created for you. (*Note*: The Advantage Diskette can be duplicated by copying all the files from your instructor's Master Advantage Diskette.)

CREATING REPORTS WITH THE REPORT WIZARD

In the next few sections, you will use the Report Wizard to create reports. Using the Report Wizard tool, you can create the following types of reports:

- *Single-Column.*
  The field values for each record are displayed down a column. Each value displays on a separate line with the field label to the left. Records are displayed one after another down the page.

- *Groups/Totals.*
  Data is organized into groups in a table format (composed of rows and columns). You can then calculate subtotals for each group and a grand total for all groups. Figure 4.1 shows an example of a Groups/Totals report that is grouped on the City field; no calculations were performed.

Figure 4.1

Grouped report

Students

26-May-94

City	Last Name	First Name	Company	Phone
Los Angeles				
	Keller	Robert	Toys for the Ageless!	213-111-1111
Redding				
	Adams	Jake	Calton Plastics	916-999-9999
	Chabot	Evelyn	<self-employed>	916-444-4444
	Fernandez	Margarita	Tires and More	916-666-6666
	Gills	Rosalie	Tires and More	916-666-6666
Sacramento				
	Bannister	Rod	7279 Ridge Drive	916-111-1111
San Diego				
	Bingham	Wendy	Decorator's, Inc.	805-111-1111
	Gaines	Don	Decorator's, Inc.	805-111-1111
	Janovich	Rosa	Sharon Rents	805-555-5552
	Shepherd	Karen	Sharon Rents	805-555-5552
San Francisco				
	Arguello	Ahmad	<self-employed>	999-111-1111
	Hurtado	Jean	Publishing Books, Inc.	415-000-0000
	Salizar	Latham	China Imports	415-888-8888
	Yee	Jack	China Imports	415-888-8888
Stockton				
	Schuler	George	Electronic DrumWorks	209-111-1111

- *Mailing Label.*
  Data is presented in a mailing-label format and then printed on mailing label stock that you insert in your printer. You choose the format of the mailing labels. Figure 4.2 shows an example of three-column mailing labels.

Figure 4.2

Three-column
mailing labels
(partial view)

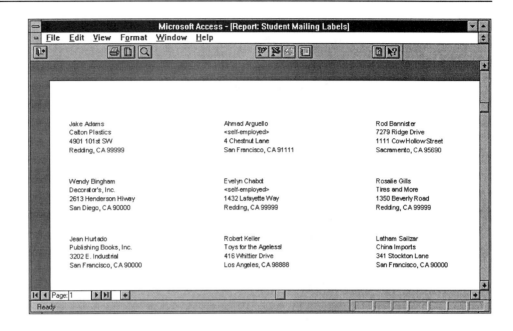

- *Summary.*
  This type of report is similar to a Groups/Totals report except that the detail records are excluded.

- *Tabular.*
  Table or query data is displayed in single columns. Labels appear at the top of each column and each row represents a new record. Access prompts you with questions that affect the final design of the report.

- *AutoReport.*
  Table or query data is displayed in single columns. This report is similar to a Tabular report, except that Access doesn't prompt you for information about the report.

- *MS Word Mailmerge.*
  Link data from a table or query to a Microsoft Word for Windows 6.0 data source file. The data can then be used to generate a report or mailing labels.

If necessary, choose File, Add-ins to use the **Add-in Manager** to change any assumptions made by the Report Wizard. For example, you might want the reports you create with the AutoReport Wizard to display in Landscape mode rather than Portrait mode. To change Report Wizard assumptions, choose File, Add-ins, Add-in Manager. Then click Form and

Report Wizards and select Customize. Finally, select a report to customize.

In the following sections you will create an AutoReport, Groups/Totals report, and a Mailing Label report.

AUTOREPORT

The **AutoReport Wizard** is the easiest Report Wizard to use because Access provides you with an AutoReport button on the Tool bar. To create a report using the AutoReport Wizard: (a) from the Database window, click Table or Query, (b) select a table or query, and (c) click the AutoReport button (🖾) on the Tool bar. Your report will display as a single-column report on the screen. (*Note*: To create any other type of report using a Report Wizard, you must click Report in the Database window, click New, select a table or query, and then select Report Wizards.)

Perform the following steps:

1. Open the TRAINING Database window.
    CLICK: 🖾
    SELECT: *the drive that contains the Advantage Diskette in the Drives*
        text box
    SELECT: TRAINING.MDB
    PRESS: (Enter) or CLICK: OK
    The Database window is displaying.

2. CLICK: Query button
    The Student Listing query name is selected.

3. CLICK: 🖾
    The screen should look similar to Figure 4.3.

Figure 4.3

This report was created using the AutoReport Wizard (partial view)

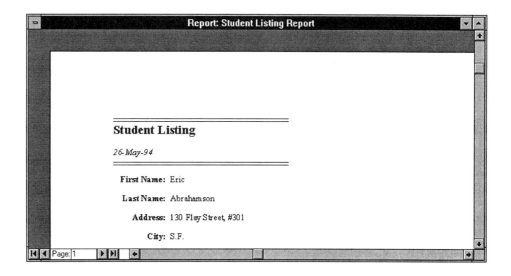

4. To zoom out so you can see more of the report:
   CLICK: Zoom button (🔍)

5. To zoom back in:
   CLICK: 🔍

6. To save the report:
   CHOOSE: File, Save As
   TYPE: Student Listing Report
   PRESS: (Enter) or CLICK: OK

7. To display the Database window:
   CHOOSE: File, Close

Quick Reference	1. In the Database window, select the Table or Query button.
Using the	2. Select a table or query.
AutoReport Wizard	3. CLICK: 🗒️
	4. PRESS: 🔍 to zoom in and out

GROUPS/TOTALS REPORT

In this section you will use a Report Wizard to create the report displaying in Figure 4.1, which groups the students by the City field. As part of defining the report, you will set the Line Spacing option to 0, which causes less space to print between each row in the report.

Perform the following steps:

1. The TRAINING Database window is displaying.

2. CLICK: Report button
    CLICK: New
    The following dialog box is displaying:

3. To select a table or query:
    CLICK: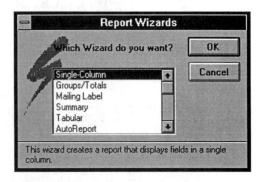
    SELECT: Students

4. CLICK: Report Wizards
    The following dialog box is displaying:

5. SELECT: Groups/Totals
    PRESS: Enter or CLICK: OK
    The dialog box pictured in Figure 4.4 should be displaying.

Figure 4.4

The initial
Groups/Totals
Report Wizard
dialog box.

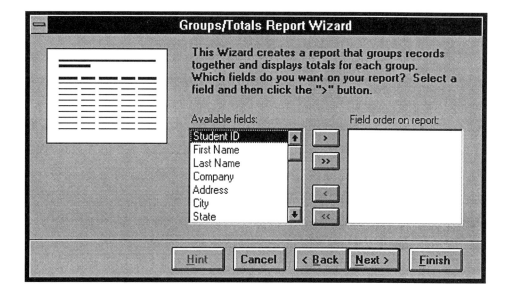

Table 4.1 describes most of the buttons you see in Figure 4.4.

Table 4.1

Report Wizard
dialog box buttons

BUTTON	PURPOSE
`>`	Select a field
`>>`	Select all fields
`<`	Remove a field
`<<`	Remove all fields
`Cancel`	Cancel current Report Wizard selections
`< Back`	Display the previous dialog box
`Next >`	Display the next dialog box
`Finish`	Display the report

6. To include the Last Name field in the report:
    SELECT: Last Name
    CLICK: `>`

7. To include the First Name field:
    SELECT: First Name
    CLICK:

8. On your own, include the Company, City, and Phone fields in the report.

9. To continue designing the report:
    CLICK: Next >

10. The Table Wizard wants to know what field to group the report by.
    SELECT: City
    CLICK: >
    CLICK: Next >

11. To accept "Normal" as the grouping selection:
    CLICK: Next >

12. The Table Wizard now wants to know what field(s) to sort on.
    SELECT: Last Name
    CLICK: >
    SELECT: First Name
    CLICK: >
    CLICK: Next >
    The dialog box in Figure 4.5 is displaying.

Figure 4.5

Choosing a style for the grouped report

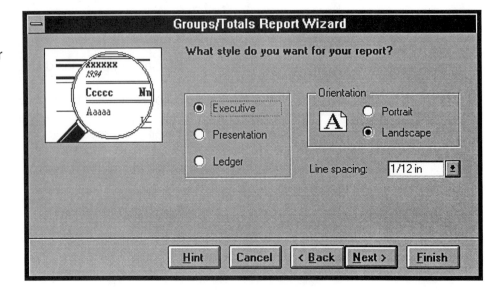

13. The available Report Wizard styles are actually very similar. The Executive and Presentation use slightly different fonts. The Ledger style displays with column and row grids.
CLICK: Presentation button

14. To change the Line spacing option:
CLICK: ⬇
CLICK: 0 in
CLICK: Next >

15. To accept the assumptions in the current dialog box:
CLICK: Finish
The zoomed-in report should be displaying on the screen.

16. To zoom the report out:
CLICK: 🔍

Quick Reference *Creating a* *Groups/Totals* *Report*	1. In the Database window: SELECT: Report button CLICK: New 2. Select a table or query. 3. CLICK: Report Wizards 4. SELECT: Groups/Totals PRESS: Enter or CLICK: OK 5. Respond to the prompts.

To save the report and then print it:

1. To save:
CHOOSE: File, Save As
TYPE: Student Listing Report
PRESS: Enter or CLICK: OK

2. To print:
CHOOSE: File, Print
PRESS: Enter or CLICK: OK

3. Close the current window so the TRAINING Database window is displaying.

MAILING LABELS REPORT

In this section, you create a mailing label report. The procedure for creating mailing labels is very similar to the one you used in the last section. In this section you will create mailing labels for the Instructors table that is stored in the TRAINING database.

Perform the following steps:

1. The TRAINING Database window is displaying.

2. CLICK: Report button
   CLICK: <u>N</u>ew

3. To select a table or query:
   CLICK:
   SELECT: Instructors

4. CLICK: Report <u>W</u>izards

5. SELECT: Mailing Label
   PRESS: [Enter] or CLICK: OK
   The dialog box pictured in Figure 4.6 is displaying.

Figure 4.6

Access is waiting for you to select fields to include in the mailing labels.

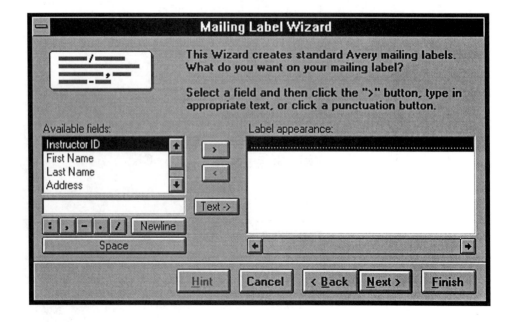

Note the additional buttons on this screen. For example, to insert a space in the mailing label, click [Space]. To insert a comma, click [,]. To begin a new line, click [Newline].

In the following steps, you will design the mailing labels:

1. To include the First Name field in the report:
    SELECT: First Name
    CLICK: [›]
    CLICK: [Space]

2. To include the Last Name field:
    SELECT: Last Name
    CLICK: [›]

3. To begin a new line and then select the Address field:
    CLICK: [Newline]
    SELECT: Address
    CLICK: [›]

4. To begin a new line and then select the City, State, and Zip fields:
    CLICK: [Newline]
    SELECT: City
    CLICK: [›]
    CLICK: [,]
    CLICK: [Space]
    SELECT: State
    CLICK: [›]
    CLICK: [Space]
    SELECT: Zip
    CLICK: [›]
    The Mailing Label Wizard dialog box should look like Figure 4.7.

Figure 4.7

The mailing label design is completed.

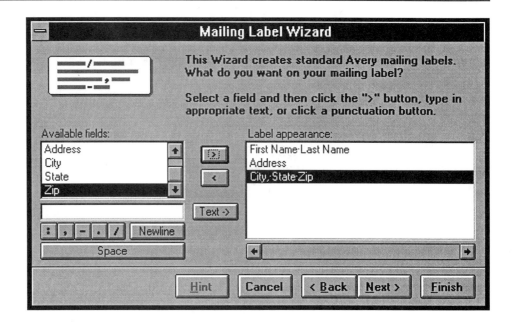

5. To continue designing the mailing labels:

   CLICK: Next >

6. You must now decide how you want the mailing labels sorted. To sort them into order by the Zip code:

   SELECT: Zip

   CLICK: >

   CLICK: Next >

7. Access lets you choose from many different mailing label formats. To accept the default format, which displays three labels across the width of the page:

   CLICK: Next >

8. Access also lets you adjust the color and font characteristics of the mailing labels. To accept the default assumptions:

   CLICK: Next >

9. To view the mailing label report on the screen:

   CLICK: Finish

   The zoomed-in report should be displaying on the screen.

10. To zoom the report out:

    CLICK: 🔍

11. To print the mailing labels:
    CHOOSE: File, Print, or
    CLICK: 🖨
    PRESS: (Enter) or CLICK: OK

12. To save the mailing label report:
    CHOOSE: File, Save
    TYPE: Instructor Mailing Labels
    PRESS: (Enter) or CLICK: OK

13. Close the current window so the Database window is displaying.

Quick Reference	1. In the Database window:
Creating a Mailing	SELECT: Report button
Labels Report	CLICK: New
	2. Select a table or query.
	3. CLICK: Report Wizards
	4. SELECT: Mailing Label
	PRESS: (Enter) or CLICK: OK
	5. Design the mailing label.
	6. Save the mailing label report.

DESIGNING A REPORT

Although Report Wizard tools provide you with an easy means of creating a variety of reports in different formats, you may find it necessary to create a report from scratch or modify the characteristics of a report that you created with the Report Wizard. For example, maybe you want less space to display between the columns in a report. Or maybe you want to include a company logo or picture in a report. Users often create the initial report layout using a Report Wizard and then modify it using one or more of the procedures described in the following sections. Before leading you through customizing a report, we need to describe the different components of a report.

UNDERSTANDING REPORTS

Reports are made up of different sections, which contain **controls** that determine what displays in the report. Access reports use two kinds of controls: bound and unbound. A **bound control** is one whose source of data is a field in a table or query. For example, an example of a bound control is one that causes the data to display in a report column; the displayed data is bound to data in a field stored in a table or query. An **unbound control** is a control that doesn't have a source of data. For example, a report title is an unbound control; you can type in the title directly.

To make the concept of controls easier to understand, you should compare a report displaying in Preview mode with one displaying in Design view.

1. Open the TRAINING database that is stored on the Advantage Diskette.

2. To preview the Instructor Listing report:
   CLICK: Report button
   CLICK: Instructor Listing
   CLICK: Preview

3. If necessary, click the Maximize button (▲) to see more of the report.

4. To zoom out:
   CLICK: 🔍
   The report should look similar to Figure 4.8.

Figure 4.8

Tabular report in Preview mode

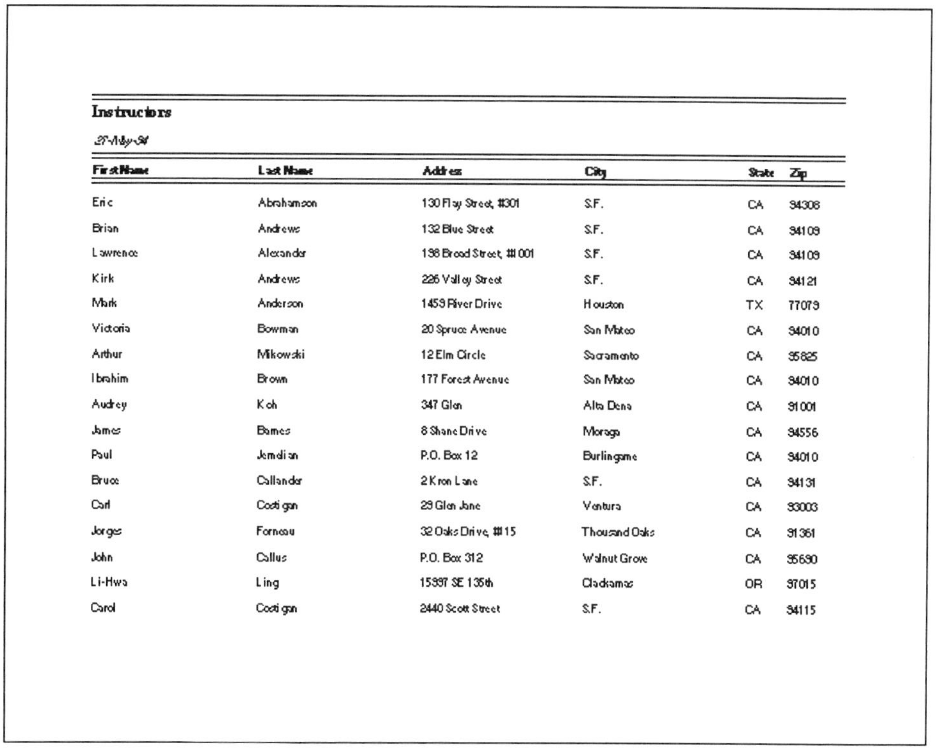

Instructors

27-May-94

FirstName	Last Name	Address	City	State	Zip
Eric	Abrahamson	130 Flay Street, #301	S.F.	CA	94308
Brian	Andrews	132 Blue Street	S.F.	CA	94109
Lawrence	Alexander	198 Broad Street, #1001	S.F.	CA	94109
Kirk	Andrews	226 Valley Street	S.F.	CA	94121
Mark	Anderson	1459 River Drive	Houston	TX	77079
Victoria	Bowman	20 Spruce Avenue	San Mateo	CA	94010
Arthur	Mikowski	12 Elm Circle	Sacramento	CA	95825
Ibrahim	Brown	177 Forest Avenue	San Mateo	CA	94010
Audrey	Koh	347 Glen	Alta Dena	CA	91001
James	Barnes	8 Shane Drive	Moraga	CA	94556
Paul	Jemdian	P.O. Box 12	Burlingame	CA	94010
Bruce	Callander	2 Kron Lane	S.F.	CA	94131
Carl	Costigan	29 Glen Jane	Ventura	CA	93003
Jorges	Forneau	32 Oaks Drive, #15	Thousand Oaks	CA	91361
John	Callus	P.O. Box 312	Walnut Grove	CA	95690
Li-Hwa	Ling	15997 SE 135th	Clackamas	OR	97015
Carol	Costigan	2440 Scott Street	S.F.	CA	94115

Although you can't read the data, you can see the general outline of the sections. The report contains the following three sections:

- *Report Header.* This section of the report contains an unbound control that displays the name of the table or query on which the report is based, and another control that causes the current date to display two lines below.

- *Page Header.* This section of the report contains unbound controls that cause column headings to display above each column of data. If four columns of data are displaying in a report, for example, then four controls, one for each heading, are included in the Page Header section.

- *Detail.* This section of the report contains the controls that are bound to the fields in the underlying table or query; these controls cause the detail data to display.

5. To display the report in Design view so you can see the Report Header, Page Header, and Detail sections:
   CHOOSE: File, Close
   The Database window should be displaying.

6. CLICK: Instructor Listing
    CLICK: Design button
    The screen should look like Figure 4.9. Notice that =*Now( )* is
    displaying in the Report Header to cause the current date to display in
    the report.

Figure 4.9

The same report in
Figure 4.8 in Design
view

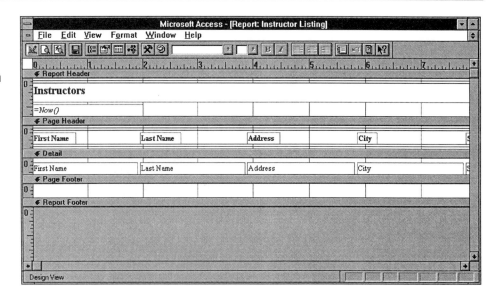

7. After you're comfortable with the different parts of a report, close the
    current window so that the TRAINING Database window is
    displaying.

In the following sections you will practice modifying some of the controls
in the Instructor Listing report. The Instructor Listing report was initially
created with the Tabular Report Wizard.

EDITING CONTROL TEXT

In this section you will edit the Report Header section of the Instructor
Listing report. The Report Header currently includes the name of the
originating table, Instructors. You're going to edit the heading to display
"Current Instructor Listing: 1995".

Perform the following steps:

1. The TRAINING Database window should be displaying.

2. To display the Instructor Listing report in Design view:
    CLICK: Report button
    CLICK: Instructor Listing
    CLICK: <u>D</u>esign
    (*Note*: If necessary, click the Maximize button (▲) to see more of the report.)

3. To select the Instructors title so you can edit it:
    POINT: to the heading "Instructors", and then
    CLICK: the left mouse button

4. To display the cursor in the title area, repeat the previous step:
    POINT: to the heading "Instructors", and then
    CLICK: the left mouse button
    The cursor should be blinking in the heading area.

5. Point and then drag the mouse over the Instructors heading in order to select it. The heading should now be displaying in reverse video.

6. TYPE: `Current Instructor Listing: 1995`
    The screen should look like Figure 4.10.

Figure 4.10

The Page Header
has been changed.

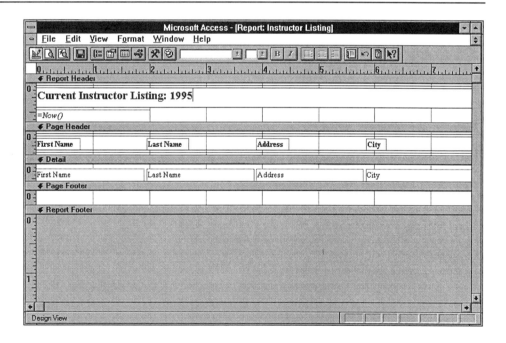

7. To save the new report design and then preview the report:
    CHOOSE: File, Save
    CLICK: Preview button ([🔍])
    The new heading should be displaying in the report.

8. To return to the Design view of the report:
    CLICK: Close Window button ([🔁])

9. Continue on to the next section to edit the Page Header.

Quick Reference	In Design view:
Editing Control Text While Viewing a Report in Design View	1. Select the control that you want to change. 2. Once a control is selected, click again until a cursor appears. Edit the text.

RESIZING CONTROLS

Notice that a lot of white space is displaying between the columns in the Instructor Listing report. To change the width of a control, you must select the control, and then drag the control border left or right to change the width.

Perform the following steps to narrow the First Name control in the Detail section:

1. If you completed the last section, the Design view of the Instructor Listing report is displaying on the screen.

2. To select the First Name control in the Detail section:
    POINT: to the First Name control in the Detail section
    CLICK: the left mouse button
    The control is selected.

You change the size of controls like you'd change the size of a window. When you point to an edge of a control, a horizontal bar with arrowheads displays. Now click and drag with the mouse in the desired direction.

3. POINT: to the right edge of the First Name control box until the pointer changes shape
    DRAG: the mouse to the left about ½ inch

(*Note*: You often have to try a few different widths before you get the width just right. After making a change, preview the report to see how it looks, then make additional changes in Design mode, if necessary.)

4. To preview the report:

   CLICK: Preview button ([🔍])
   Notice that although the column is narrower, the columns to the right have remained in their original positions. Therefore, the report looks the same as before. In the next section, we lead you through repositioning the controls in the Page Header and Detail sections.

5. To return to the Design view of the report:

   CLICK: Close Window button ([🔳])

6. On your own, narrow the Last Name and City controls in the Detail section about ½ inch.

7. If you preview the report right now, you'll see that the report doesn't look any different. Display the report in Design view and continue on to the next section to learn how to move controls.

Quick Reference	In Design view:
Resizing Controls	1. Select the control that you want to resize.
While Viewing a	2. Point to the left or right edge of the control to be resized until a
Report in Design	horizontal bar with arrowheads displays.
View	3. Drag the border to the left or right.

MOVING CONTROLS

You move a control by selecting it and then pointing to the top or bottom edge of the control until a small hand appears. When the hand appears, drag the control in the desired direction.

Perform the following steps to move the Last Name control to the left:

1. SELECT: Last Name control in the Detail section

2. POINT: to the top border of the control until a hand displays
   DRAG: the control to the left about ½ inch

3. Using the procedure described in steps 1–2, move the Address, City, State, and Zip fields to the left so that each is close to the field control on the left.

4. CLICK: Preview button (⬚)
   Notice that the Page Header controls aren't displaying above the Detail controls.

5. CLICK: Close Window button (⬚)

6. On your own, move each Page Header control to display above the corresponding Detail control field.

7. CLICK: Preview button (⬚)
   The report should look similar to Figure 4.11. In the next section, you learn how to display an unbound graphic control in a report.

Figure 4.11

The controls in the Detail section have been narrowed and the controls in the Page Header and Detail sections have been moved to the left.

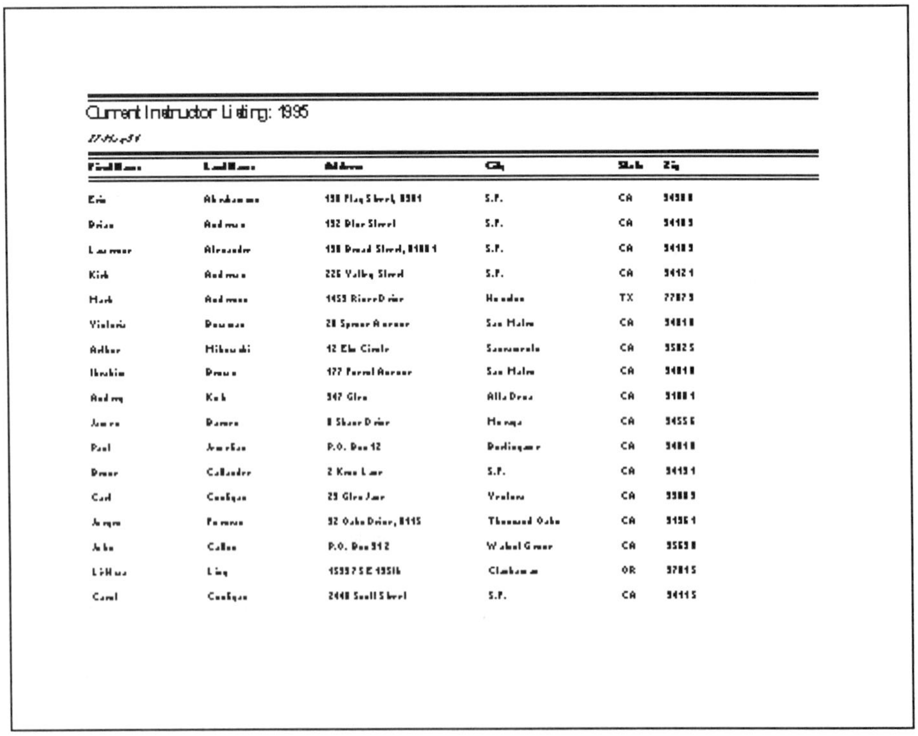

8. To save the new report design and then display the report in Design view:

    CHOOSE: File, Save

    CLICK: Close Window button ()

9. Continue on to the next section to add a graphic to the report.

Quick Reference	In Design view:
Moving a Control While Viewing a Report in Design View	1. Select the control that you want to move.
	2. Point to the top or bottom of the control until a small hand displays.
	3. Drag the control in the desired direction.

ADDING A GRAPHIC TO A REPORT

In this section, you are going to embed an unbound graphic object into the Instructor Listing report that is stored in the TRAINING database. The name of the graphic is BOOKS.BMP and is stored on the Advantage Diskette. You will insert the graphic into the Report Header. Since this is an unbound object, the object will only print on the first page of the report (Figure 4.12). If you insert the graphic in the Detail section, the graphic will print with every record (Figure 4.13).

Figure 4.12

The Instructor Listing report after a graphic control was inserted in the Report Header

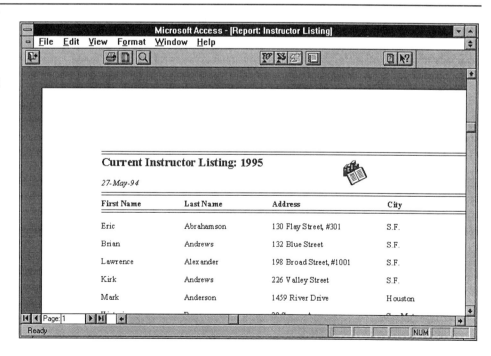

Figure 4.13

The Instructor
Listing report after a
graphic control was
inserted in the
Detail section

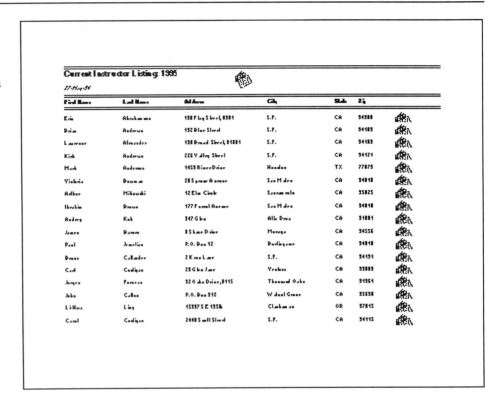

Perform the following steps:

1. If you completed the last section, the Design view of the Instructor Listing report is displaying on the screen.

2. If necessary, click the Maximize button (▲) to see more of the report.

3. To display the Toolbox tools:
    CHOOSE: View, Toolbox

4. Drag the mouse slowly over the Tool bar and notice that a description of each button displays.

5. To insert a frame into which you can put an object:
    CLICK: Object Frame button (▣)
    In the next step you must tell Access where to position the frame. You will position it to the right of the Report Header text.

6. Point to the right of "1995" in the Report Header in the 4-inch position, approximately; you are currently pointing to the upper-left corner of the frame you are about to insert. Click and drag down and to the right

(to position 5-inch, approximately) in order to create a frame. Release the mouse button.

7. The dialog box, shown below, is displaying. Access is waiting for you to tell it more about the object you're about to insert.

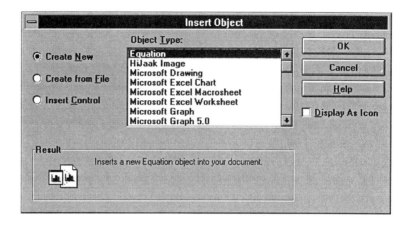

CLICK: Create from File
The following dialog box is displaying:

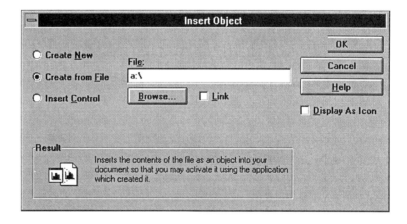

8. Click to the right of the "a:\" in the File text box so that a cursor displays.

9. TYPE: books.bmp
PRESS: (Enter) or CLICK: OK

10. So that the Toolbox doesn't display:
CHOOSE: View, Toolbox
In Design view, the report should look like Figure 4.14.

Figure 4.14

Design view. A
graphic control was
inserted in the
Report Header of
the Instructor
Listing report.

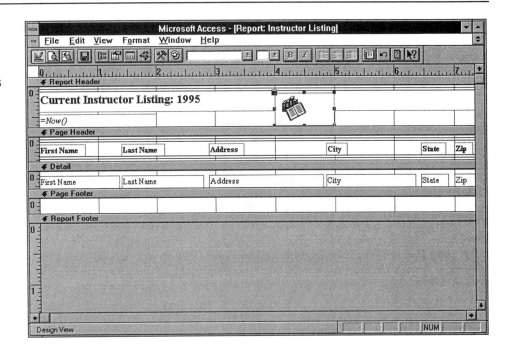

11. To view the report:
    CLICK: Preview button (image)
    The report should look like Figure 4.12.

12. To save the report:
    CHOOSE: File, Save

13. Close the current window so that the TRAINING Database window is
    displaying.

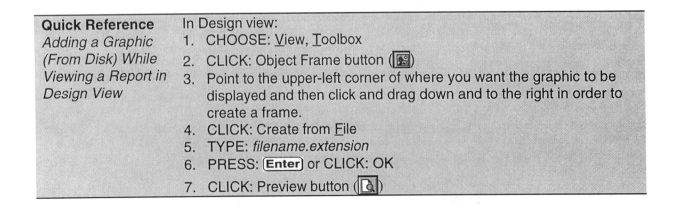

Quick Reference	In Design view:
Adding a Graphic (From Disk) While Viewing a Report in Design View	1. CHOOSE: View, Toolbox
	2. CLICK: Object Frame button (image)
	3. Point to the upper-left corner of where you want the graphic to be displayed and then click and drag down and to the right in order to create a frame.
	4. CLICK: Create from File
	5. TYPE: *filename.extension*
	6. PRESS: (Enter) or CLICK: OK
	7. CLICK: Preview button (image)

SUMMARY

In this session you learned how to create reports using Report Wizards. Report Wizard tools simplify the process of creating a report by making formatting assumptions about the completed report. The AutoReport Wizard is the easiest Report Wizard to use. You simply select a table form the Database window and then click the AutoReport button (🖉) on the Tool bar.

You also learned how to create a reports without the aid of a Report Wizard tool. Reports are made up of different sections, including the Report Header, Page Header, and Detail sections. The Report Header prints at the very beginning and end of the report. For example, the report title and summary statistics are commonly displayed in the Report Header section. The Page Header prints at the top and bottom of each page. For example, the current date or page number might display on the top or bottom of each page. The Detail section displays the report data. Each report section contains controls which can be modified (deleted, resized, moved) to meet your needs.

COMMAND SUMMARY

Table 4.2 provides a list of the commands and procedures covered in this session.

Table 4.2	*COMMAND*	*TASK*
Command Summary	🖉	AutoReport Wizard button
	🔍	In Preview mode, zoom in and out
	In the Database window, click Report button, New, Report Wizards, select a table or query, select a report format	Use a Report Wizard to create a report
	While viewing a report in Design view, select a control and then click on the control again. Edit the text.	Edit control text

While viewing a report in Design view, select a control, point to the left or right edge of the control until the bar with arrowheads appears, drag the border left or right.	Resize controls
While viewing a report in Design view, select a control, point to the top or bottom of the control until a small hand displays, drag the control in the desired direction.	Move a control
In Design view, View, Toolbox, [icon], point to where the frame should be positioned and then click and drag to the right and down, Create from File, *filename.extension*, Enter	Add a graphic (from disk) to a report

KEY TERMS

Add-in Manager   Using this tool, you can change the default display assumptions made by the Report Wizard.

AutoReport Wizard   Using this tool, you can have Access create a single-column report without requesting any information from you. The AutoReport Wizard can be accessed from clicking [icon] on the Tool Bar.

bound control   In Access, a control whose source of data is a field in a table or query.

control   An element of a report. Access uses two types of controls: *bound* and *unbound*.

report   In Access, a report is used to improve the appearance of table or query data so it can be included in a presentation.

Report Wizard   An Access tool that simplifies the process of creating a report. You select the type of report and then respond to prompts.

unbound control   In Access, a control that doesn't have a source of data; you can type the control information in directly.

EXERCISES

SHORT ANSWER

1. What must you do before you use the AutoReport button to create a report?
2. When might you want to use the Add-in Manager?
3. What is the difference between a single-column report and a tabular report?
4. What is a bound control? unbound control?
5. In a printed report, where would you find the report header, page header, and detail sections?
6. In general, describe the process of including a graphic in a report.
7. How do you change control text?
8. How do you move a control?
9. How to you resize a control?
10. When might you want to use a groups/totals report?

HANDS-ON

(*Note*: In the following exercises, save your work onto and open files from the Advantage Diskette.)

1. To practice using the AutoReport Wizard, create an AutoReport for the Customer table that is stored in the SPORTING database. When finished, save the report onto the disk as "Customer AutoReport."

2. Use the Report Wizard to create mailing labels for the Customer table that is stored in the SPORTING database.
   a. The field layout for the mailing labels should look like the following:

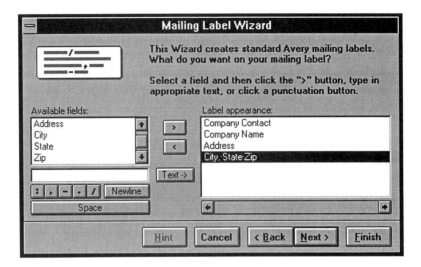

b. Sort the labels by the Zip field.
c. Use the default label size.
d. Use the default font and color settings.
e. Save the labels as "Customer Mailing Labels".
f. Print the mailing labels.

3. To practice creating and editing a report, perform the following steps using the Customer table of the SPORTING database:
   a. Use the Report Wizard to create a tabular report. When selecting fields, refer to the following dialog box:

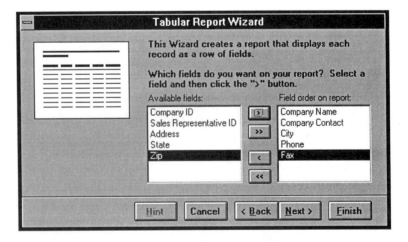

   b. Sort the report on the City field.
   c. Assume the default style and title settings.
   d. Save the report as "Complete Customer Listing".
   e. Edit the report by resizing the City, Phone, and Fax fields so they are narrower.
   f. Move the Phone and Fax fields to the left so they are closer to the adjacent field.

    g. In the Page Header, move the City, Phone, and Fax titles so they line up above the corresponding field controls in the Detail section.

    h. Edit the Report Header text to read "1995 Customer Listing".

    i. Save the report.

    j. Print the report.

4. To practice including a graphic to a report, add the PHONE.BMP picture, stored on the Advantage Diskette, to the report you created in exercise 3 named "Complete Customer Listing." The graphic should display in the Report Header section. Save and print the report.

SESSION 5

MICROSOFT ACCESS 2.0 FOR WINDOWS: ADVANCED TOPICS

In this session, you learn a few techniques to make you more productive when working with Access. You learn how to create a form with the Form Wizard and then modify it to include features that simplify the data entry process. You also learn how to create a command button which you can use to streamline your interaction with a database application.

PREVIEW

When you have completed this session, you will be able to:

Use the Form Wizard to create a form that includes a subform.

•

Edit a form by:

Deleting and repositioning controls.
Displaying values in a list.
Changing the tab order.
Setting default values.

•

Create and test a command button.

Why Is This Session Important?
Creating Forms
       Creating a Subform
       Deleting and Repositioning Controls
       Displaying Values in a List
       Changing Tab Order
       Setting Default Values
Creating a Command Button
       Testing the Command Button
Summary
       Command Summary
Key Terms
Exercises
       Short Answer
       Hands-On

WHY IS THIS SESSION IMPORTANT?

Having completed the first four sessions of this guide, you are now capable of working with Microsoft Access quite comfortably. However, there are many features of Access that we have not yet introduced. In this session, you will create a form with the Form Wizard tool and then edit the form to include additional features that will help you to use Access more reliably and with less effort. You will also learn how to create command buttons which help you to automate frequently used procedures. The overall objective of this session is to familiarize you with some different aspects of Access to provide a foundation for further exploration.

Before proceeding, make sure the following are true:

1. You have loaded Microsoft Access for Windows.
2. Your Advantage Diskette is inserted into drive A: or drive B:. You will save your work onto the diskette and retrieve files that have been created for you. (*Note*: The Advantage Diskette can be duplicated by copying all the files from your instructor's Master Advantage Diskette.)

CREATING FORMS

In Session 2, you created a form using the AutoForm Wizard (), which automatically created a form for you without asking you any questions. In this section you learn about the different types of forms that you can create with a Form Wizard and how to edit forms. Many of the editing techniques you used to edit reports can be used when editing forms. For example, you select, move, and resize controls using the same techniques.

Using the Form Wizard tool, you can create the following types of forms:

- *Single-Column*. The field values for each record are displayed down a column. Each value displays on a separate line with the field label to the left. Figure 5.1 provides an example of a single-column form.

Figure 5.1

Single-column form

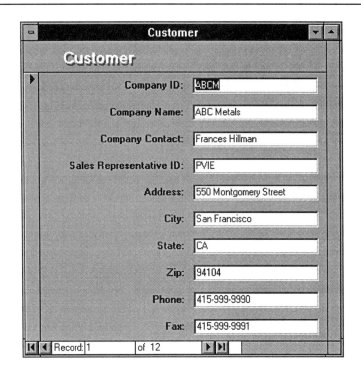

- *Tabular*. Record values are displayed left to right across the page. Labels appear at the top of each column and each row represents a new record. Figure 5.2 provides an example of a tabular form; you use (Tab) to see additional fields.

Figure 5.2

Tabular form

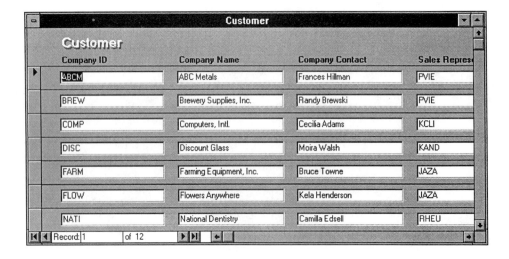

- *Graph*. Microsoft Access comes with Microsoft Graph, an OLE application that enables you to graph your Access data. Use this type of form to graph numeric data in the form of a pie graph, line graph, or three-dimensional column graph.

- *Main/Subform*. To include data from more than one table on a form, use a **subform**, which is a form within a form. In Access, the primary form is referred to as the Main form and the form within that is the subform. Figure 5.3 provides an example of a form that contains a subform. From the SPORTING database, the main form is based on the Customer table and the subform (the table below) is based on the Sales Representatives table. With this setup, you can enter Sales Representative ID data into the Customer table by referring to the subform below.

Figure 5.3

Main/subform

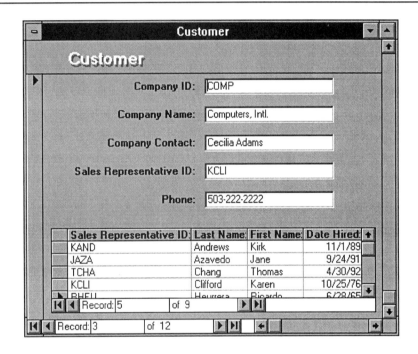

- *AutoForm*. An Access tool that automatically creates a single-column form for you without prompting you for information. After selecting a table or query in the Database window, click [icon] to create an AutoForm.

If necessary, choose File, Add-ins to use the Add-in Manager to change any assumptions made by the Form Wizard. For example, you might want the form you create with the AutoForm Wizard to display in a different style (example: Shadowed instead of Embossed). To change Form Wizard assumptions, choose File, Add-ins, Add-in Manager. Then click Form and Report Wizards and select Customize. Finally, select a form to customize.

CREATING A SUBFORM

In this section you will open the WEDDING database and then use the Form Wizard to create a form that contains a subform. The main form is the Gifts table and the subform is the Guest List table. Once you complete the form, you will refer to the subform data in order to enter Guest ID data into the Gifts table. You will modify the form in subsequent sections to include additional features.

Perform the following steps:

1. Open the WEDDING database.

2. The WEDDING Database window should be displaying. To create a new form:
    CLICK: Form button
    CLICK: New

3. The New Form dialog box is displaying. To select a table or query:
    CLICK: [↓]
    SELECT: Gifts

4. CLICK: Form Wizards
    The following dialog box is displaying:

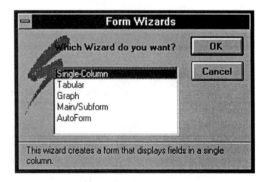

5. SELECT: Main/Subform
    PRESS: [Enter] or CLICK: OK
    Access is waiting for you to designate the source of the subform.

6. To select the Guest List table as the subform data source:
   CLICK: Guest List
   CLICK: | Next > |

7. To select fields to include on the main form (from the Gifts table):
   CLICK: | >> | *to select all fields*
   CLICK: | Next > |

8. To select fields to include on the subform (from the Guest List table):
   CLICK: Guest ID
   CLICK: | > |
   CLICK: Last Name
   CLICK: | > |
   CLICK: First Name
   CLICK: | > |
   CLICK: | Next > |

9. To accept the default style:
   CLICK: | Next > |

10. To accept the default title:
    CLICK: | Finish |
    After a few seconds, you will get a message requiring you to save the subform before continuing.
    CLICK: OK
    TYPE: Guest ID Listing
    PRESS: [Enter] or CLICK: OK

11. Access will display another message indicating it couldn't establish a link between the form and the subform. Since you don't need them to have a link:
    CLICK: OK
    The Gifts form should be displaying (Figure 5.4). (*Note*: If necessary, increase the size of the Form window so you can see the subform displaying on the bottom of the form.) This form will be especially useful when you need to enter a new record to the Gifts table; when one of your guests gives you a gift, you can refer to the subform to obtain the correct Guest ID for input into the Gifts table.

Figure 5.4

The subform
provides Guest ID
information needed
to enter new
records in the Gifts
table.

12. CLICK: *in the subform datasheet area*
    PRESS: ⬇ *continuously*
    Notice that records scroll in the subform area. (*Note*: You can't edit subform records.)

13. To save the new form:
    CHOOSE: File, Save Form
    TYPE: Gifts Main/Subform
    PRESS: Enter or CLICK: OK

14. To display the Database window:
    CHOOSE: File, Close

DELETING AND REPOSITIONING CONTROLS

Each control on your form has an attached label. You can delete the control and the attached label at once by selecting the control text box and then pressing Delete. To delete only the attached label, select the label and press Delete.

In this section you will delete the Category field from the Gifts Main/Subform and then reposition all the controls and their attached labels so that less room displays between them. When finished, the form will look like Figure 5.5. (*Note*: You will use this modified form in the next section.)

Figure 5.5

A field has been deleted from the form and the vertical spacing was changed.

Perform the following steps:

1. The WEDDING Database window should be displaying.
   CLICK: Form button
   SELECT: Gifts Main/Subform
   CLICK: Design button

2. SELECT: Category text box
   Note: Both the text box and the corresponding label are automatically selected.

3. To delete the Category text box and the associated label:
   PRESS: Delete

4. You must now select all the controls and their associated labels by doing the following:
   POINT: to the 0-inch mark on the ruler to the left of the Detail section
   DRAG: the mouse down to just below the Where Purchased field and then release the mouse button
   All the fields in the Detail section should be selected.

5. To align the selected fields vertically with less space between them:
   CHOOSE: Format, Vertical Spacing
   CHOOSE: Decrease
   To decrease the space again:
   CHOOSE: Format, Vertical Spacing
   CHOOSE: Decrease

6. To save the form and then display the Database window:
   CHOOSE: File, Save
   CHOOSE: File, Close

7. To view the form:
   SELECT: Gifts Main/Subform
   CLICK: Open button
   The form should look like Figure 5.5.

8. Close the form to display the Database window.

Quick Reference *Deleting Controls*	While viewing the form in Design view: 1. To delete a text box control and the attached label, select the text box control and press `Delete`. 2. To delete only an attached label, select the label and press `Delete`.

Quick Reference *Changing the Vertical Spacing Between Controls*	While viewing the form in Design view: 1. Select the controls you want to reposition by dragging the mouse along the ruler on the left side of the Detail section of the form. 2. CHOOSE: Format, Vertical Spacing 3. CHOOSE: Make Equal, Increase, or Decrease

In the next section you will re-insert the Category control in the form of a list box.

DISPLAYING VALUES IN A LIST

In this section you will edit the form in Figure 5.5 to look like Figure 5.6. Using the new form, the user will be able to select an option from the Category list in order to input a value.

Figure 5.6

The form with a list box

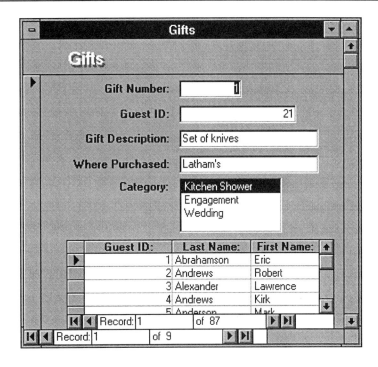

Perform the following steps:

1. The WEDDING Database window should be displaying.
   CLICK: Form button
   SELECT: Gifts Main/Subform
   CLICK: Design button

2. To add a list box to the form:
   CHOOSE: View
   If a check isn't displaying next to the Control Wizards option:
   CHOOSE: Control Wizards
   Otherwise, click on an unused area of the Application window.

3. CLICK: List Box tool in the toolbox ( )

4. To draw the list box border, point to the upper-left corner of where you want to position the list box and then drag with the mouse to the right and down. (*Note*: Refer to Figure 5.6.) Then release the mouse button.

5. Access now wants to know where to get the list box values.
    CLICK: I will type in the values that I want
    CLICK: Next >

6. So that the list box contains one column:
    TYPE: 1

7. CLICK: *in the Col1 text box*

8. TYPE: Kitchen Shower
    PRESS: ↓
    TYPE: Engagement
    PRESS: ↓
    TYPE: Wedding
    The List Box Wizard dialog should look similar to Figure 5.7.

Figure 5.6

Defining the contents of a list box

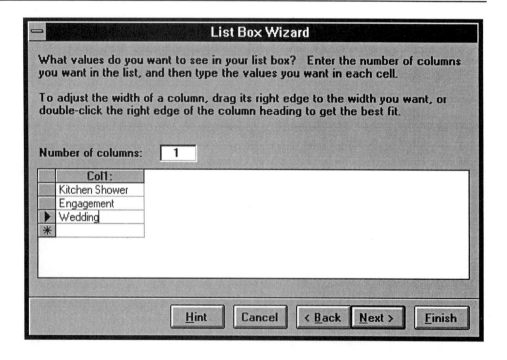

9. To move to the next screen:
    CLICK: Next >

10. CLICK: Store that value in this field
    CLICK: [⬇]
    SELECT: Category
    The user's selection will be stored in the Category field.
    CLICK: [Next >]

11. To name the list box:
    TYPE: Category:
    CLICK: [Finish]

12. The form should be displaying in Design view. Notice that the control for the Category label isn't wide enough to display the text.
    SELECT: the Category label
    POINT: to the left side of the label box until a horizontal bar with arrowheads displays
    DRAG: the mouse to the left until you think the box is wide enough and then release the mouse button

13. To save the form and then display the Database window:
    CHOOSE: File, Save
    CHOOSE: File, Close

14. To view the form:
    SELECT: Gifts Main/Subform
    CLICK: Open button
    The form should look like Figure 5.6.

To practice using the form, perform the following steps:

1. To display the first blank record:
   CLICK: [▶] *on the bottom edge of the Form window*
   CLICK: [▶] *on the bottom edge of the Form window*

2. To enter the Guest ID:
   PRESS: [Tab]
   You need to enter Audrey Koh's Guest ID.
   CLICK: *in the subform datasheet area*
   PRESS: [↓] *until Audrey Koh's name displays and take note of her Guest ID number*
   CLICK: *in the Guest ID field of the main form*
   PRESS: [Delete]
   TYPE: *Audrey Koh's Guest ID number*
   PRESS: [Tab]

3. To continue filling in the record:
    TYPE: Barbeque Tools
    PRESS: (Tab)
    TYPE: Monde Boutique
    PRESS: (Tab)
    Notice that the cursor moves to the subform instead of to the Category field. You will correct this in the next section.

4. Continue on to the next section so you can learn about changing the tab order of the fields on the form.

Quick Reference	While displaying the form in Design view

Display Values in a List (you type in the list box values)	1. CHOOSE: View, Control Wizards to display the toolbox
	    CLICK: List Box tool (🔳)
	2. To draw the list box border, point to the upper-left corner of where you want to position the list box and then drag with the mouse to the right and down. Release the mouse button.
	3. CLICK: I will type in the values that I want
	    CLICK: Next >
	4. Type in the number of columns and then fill in the table.
	    CLICK: Next >
	5. CLICK: Store that value in this field
	    SELECT: a field into which the list box value should be stored
	    CLICK: Next >
	6. TYPE: *a label for the list box*
	    CLICK: Finish

CHANGING TAB ORDER

If you completed the steps so far in this lesson, you now have a form that is almost complete. You must now tell Access where to move the cursor when you press (Tab). Currently, when you press (Tab) with the cursor in the Where Purchased field, the cursor jumps to the subform (instead of to the Category field).

1. The Form window is displaying.
    CHOOSE: View, Form Design

2. CHOOSE: Edit, Tab Order
    The Tab Order dialog box should look similar to the following:

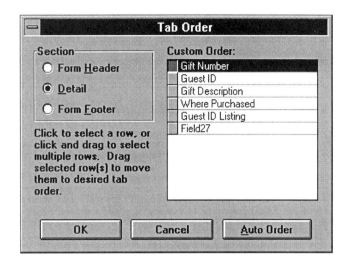

Notice that the Guest ID Listing subform name is listing after the Where Purchased field in the list. Also, a field named Field# (for example, Field25 or Field27) is listing last. (*Note*: Field# is an internal name that Access has given to the Category list box.)

3. SELECT: the Field27 row
    DRAG: the Field27 row so it will display above the Guest ID Listing
        field; release the mouse button
    Field27 should now be listing after the Where Purchased field in the
    Tab Order dialog box.
    CLICK: OK

4. To display the form:
    CLICK: Form view button (⊞)

5. To complete the entry of the record you started entering in the last
    section:
    CLICK: ▶ *on the bottom edge of the Form window*
    The Barbeque Tools record should be displaying.

6. To see if the tab order has changed:
    PRESS: Tab *four times*
    The cursor should now be positioned in the Category field.

7. To accept Kitchen Shower as the Category type:
    CLICK: Kitchen Shower
    PRESS: Enter

8. To enter data into the next record:
    CLICK: ▶ on the bottom edge of the Form window

9. To save the form and then close the window:
   CHOOSE: File, Save Form
   CHOOSE: File, Close

Quick Reference	While displaying the form in Design view:
Change the Tab	1. CHOOSE: Edit, Tab Order
Order	2. SELECT: the field you want to move
	3. DRAG: the field to the new position
	CLICK: OK

SETTING DEFAULT VALUES

When adding table records, you may find that you're typing the same data repeatedly into a particular field. For example, wedding guests are purchasing many gifts at "The Napa Kitchen." Wouldn't it be nice if Access would automatically fill in "The Napa Kitchen" in the Where Purchased field of the Gifts table? Then, you only need to type in an entry if a gift comes from a different location.

Perform the following steps to include "The Napa Kitchen" as the default value for the Where Purchased field:

1. The WEDDING Database window should be displaying.
   CLICK: Form button
   SELECT: Gifts Main/Subform
   CLICK: Open

2. CHOOSE: View, Form Design

3. SELECT: Where Purchased text box control

4. CHOOSE: View, Properties
   The properties for the Where Purchased text box should be displaying (Figure 5.8). As you can see, using the Properties box, you can control almost every aspect of a field. Not only can you establish a default value for a field, but you can control such things as what happens when the user makes a data entry mistake, and what happens when you press (Enter).

Figure 5.8

Properties that
relate to the Where
Purchased control
(partial list)

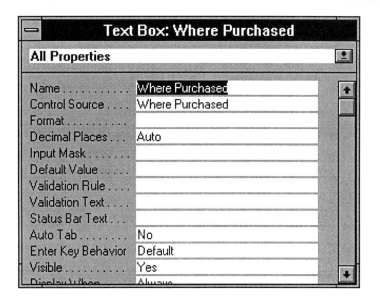

5. To establish a default value for the Where Purchased field:
   CLICK: Default Value row
   TYPE: The Napa Kitchen
   PRESS: (Enter)

6. To close the Properties window:
   DOUBLE-CLICK: Application control menu (☐)

7. To display the form:
   CHOOSE: View, Form

8. To display the first blank record:
   CLICK: 🢒🢒 *on the bottom edge of the Form window*
   CLICK: 🢒 *on the bottom edge of the Form window*
   Notice that "The Napa Kitchen" is displaying in the Where Purchased
   field.

9. Close the Form window so that the WEDDING Database window is
   displaying.

Quick Reference   While displaying the form in Design view:
Setting a Default   1. SELECT: a text box control
Value   2. CHOOSE: View, Properties
                       3. CLICK: Default Value row
                       4. TYPE: the default data
                          PRESS: (Enter)
                       5. DOUBLE-CLICK: Application control menu (☐)

CREATING A COMMAND BUTTON

In this section you learn how to create a **command button**, which is used to automatically perform an action for you so that your database is easier to use. For example, suppose you're using a form to enter data into the Students table that is stored in the TRAINING database. What if you want to simply click a button to preview a status report on the screen? You can do this by creating a command button on the form. When clicked, the action you specify (i.e., display the status report) is carried out. In the following steps you will create the command button pictured in Figure 5.9.

Figure 5.9

Form with a Student Report command button. When clicked, the Student Listing Report will display in Preview mode.

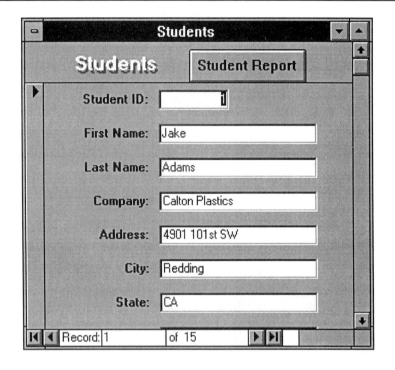

1. Open the TRAINING database.

2. CLICK: Form button
    SELECT: Student Entry Form
    CLICK: Design

3. To display the toolbox:
   CHOOSE: View
   If a check isn't displaying next to the Control Wizards option:
   CHOOSE: Control Wizards
   Otherwise, click on an unused area of the Application window.

4. To create a command button:
   CLICK: Command button tool (🔲)

5. Click an empty area of the Student Entry Form. For example, click to the right of Students in the Form Header (see Figure 5.9).

6. The first Command Button Wizard dialog box should be displaying. Under "Categories:"
   CLICK: Report Operations

7. Under "When button is pressed:"
   CLICK: Preview Report
   CLICK: Next >

8. To choose the report to preview:
   CLICK: Student Listing Report
   CLICK: Next >

9. To specify the text that you want to display on the command button:
   CLICK: Text button
   CLICK: in the Text text box
   PRESS: Home
   PRESS: Delete until the text is deleted
   TYPE: Student Report
   CLICK: Finish

10. Continue on to the next section to test the command button.

TESTING THE COMMAND BUTTON

If you completed the last section, the Student Entry Form should be displaying in Design view.

1. CHOOSE: View, Form
   The form should look similar to Figure 5.9.

2. CLICK: Student Report button
   After a few seconds, the Student Listing Report will display on the screen in Preview mode.

3. Click 🔍 to zoom the display or 🖨 to print the report. When finished, click 🔁 to display the form.

4. To save the form and then display the Database window:
   CHOOSE: File, Save Form
   CHOOSE: File, Close

5. To close the TRAINING database:
   CHOOSE: File, Close Database

Quick Reference	While displaying the form in Design view:
Create a Command Button	1. CHOOSE: View, Control Wizards
	2. CLICK: Command button tool (▢)
	3. To position the command button, click an empty area of the form.
	4. Select a category and an action to perform when the button is pressed.
	5. Select the object to open.
	6. CLICK: Text button
	7. Into the Text box, type the text you want to display on the button.
	8. CLICK: Finish

SUMMARY

This session introduced you to some advanced Access topics, including customizing forms and creating command buttons. In the first part of the session, you created a form that contained a subform. You then edited the form to reposition the text controls and their labels, include a list box, and change the tab order. You learned that by choosing View, Properties to display the field properties for a selected control, you can control the characteristics of a field in a form.

In the last part of the session, you learned how to create a command button. Command buttons are used to automate frequently used procedures and can save you much time when working with Access on an ongoing basis.

COMMAND SUMMARY

Table 5.1 provides a list of the commands and procedures covered in this session.

Table 5.1	*COMMAND*	*TASK*
Command Summary	While viewing a form in Design view, select a text box and/or label and then press (Delete).	Delete controls
	Format, Vertical Spacing	Change the vertical spacing between controls
	View, Control Wizards, ▦, follow the screen prompts	Display values in a list
	Edit, Tab Order	Change the tab order
	View, Properties	View field properties
	View, Control Wizards, ▣, follow the screen prompts	Create a command button

KEY TERMS

command button   A tool you create to automate frequently used procedures.

subform   A form within a form.

EXERCISES

SHORT ANSWER

1. What is the difference between a single-column form and a tabular form?

2. What is a subform?
3. Provide an example of when it would be useful to use a subform.
4. While viewing a form in Design view, how do you delete an Access control?
5. On a form, when might you want to view items in a list?
6. What is a command button?
7. What does it mean to change the tab order on a form?
8. What is the relationship between a main form and a subform?
9. What is a graph form?
10. When would you want to give a field a default value?

HANDS-ON

(*Note*: In the following exercises, save your work onto and retrieve files from the Advantage Diskette.)

1. Create a single-column form named for the Sales Representatives table of the SPORTING database that looks like the following:

Save the form as "Sales Reps".

2. Edit the Sales Reps form of the SPORTING database so that it looks like the following:

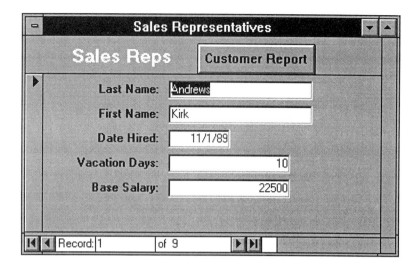

Make sure to:

a. Include less vertical space.

b. Include a command button that displays the "Complete Customer Listing" report. (*Note*: You created this report in Session 4 Hands-On exercise 3.)

c. Test the command button.

d. Save the form.